Francis Tuite

Ireland's Revolt in '98

With sketches of prominent statesmen and the social condition of the people

Francis Tuite

Ireland's Revolt in '98

With sketches of prominent statesmen and the social condition of the people

ISBN/EAN: 9783337323875

Printed in Europe, USA, Canada, Australia, Japan

Cover: Foto ©ninafisch / pixelio.de

More available books at **www.hansebooks.com**

Ireland's Revolt in '98,

WITH

Sketches of Prominent Statesmen

AND

The Social Condition of the People,

BY

F. TUITE.

BOSTON:
ANGEL GUARDIAN PRESS,
1898

INTRODUCTION.

The historian of every nation finds a considerable part of his work in recounting and explaining revolutions. Great Britain has furnished its share of them. The most thrilling military records of England are found in the numerous insurrectionary movements of its people. If Ireland presents the same interesting features from time to time it need not strike anyone as strange. But the latest rebellion of any serious import in that country, breaking out in 1798, has a special interest both for the compatriots and descendants of those who took part in it and for the general public, who sympathize with any people in arms to recover their liberty.

It was a break for freedom made by a people long provoked by oppressive foreign legislation, and robbed of their possessions in the name of law.

It was rash, no doubt, on account of insufficient preparation and the limited resources at the command of the rebels. Like all unsuccessful rebellions, it brought heavier chains and additional measures of repression on the country. But it was a new proof of the folly of a ruling power hoping to wholly stamp out the spirit of resistance against wrong.

Through those one hundred years now past since the event the same spirit of revolt against tyranny has continued, silent, indeed, and partly suppressed; and it is still there as fresh as ever ready to burst forth anew whenever a favorable opportunity is offered. So powerless is physical force against conscience, or unjust legislation against the noble aspirations of a people determined to be free!

Every sincere friend of the people deplores the existence of this revolutionary tendency and would counsel moderate methods of seeking redress of grievances. Yet this spirit of revolt will cease only when statesmen will condescend to legislate in the interest of the dependent classes as well as of the aristocracy, and thus remove the cause of discontent.

In our youth we heard our grandfathers tell those stories of bloodshed—of an armed peasantry battling against regular English troops —of brave charges—of victories won; and then, of final surrender and defeat.

The writer recalls many earnest conversations held on winter evenings during boyhood, as the family groups assembled about the cheerful fire. We, garrulous youths, drew from our aged parents those tales of troubled times. We listened with willing ears, and often with throbbing hearts, as the narrative led us through battlefields, or well-planned sieges, told by those who were themselves eye witnesses of the scenes, or actually took part in them.

Our young minds could not conceive the need of those hangings of rebels; not to speak of other more barbarous inflictions, that followed their defeat. We would often ask, "Would not a penalty less severe be enough for any government in order to keep down rebellion?"

What appeared then so unnecessary and so cruel has not changed since to our minds in its barbarous features. After a period of forty years passed since we heard the story we still pronounce it monstrous to sacrifice human life so needlessly.

But, as history shows, in every country and age, a tyrannous power needs to perpetuate itself by measures even more opposed to reason and moderation and more revolting to humanity than the act of rebellion itself.

While there is much to discourage the student of the past, we try to persuade ourselves, and we earnestly hope, that the occasion will never again arise for a repetition of such disastrous conflicts, and that future governments, following a more humane policy in legislation, will remove all causes of dissension in the community and whatever tends to excite the wild passions of the multitude.

CONTENTS.

	PAGE
Introduction	5
Contents	9
Chapter I—Agitation Preceding the Rebellion	11
Chapter II—Causes of Discontent	21
Chapter III—Efforts to Secure Foreign Aid	26
Chapter IV—Conflict Begun	33
Chapter V—Battles at New Ross, Arklow, and Vinegar Hill	44
Chapter VI—Some Battles in Ulster	50
Chapter VII—Aid from France Arrives	52
Chapter VIII—Battle of Ballinamuck	62
Chapter IX—Other Expeditions from France	65
Chapter X—Fate of the Leaders	67
Chapter XI—Prominent Statesmen of the Time	86
Chapter XII—The Union of Ireland with Great Britain	101
Chapter XIII—Causes of Dissension among Irish Patriots	121
Concluding Hints	151

IRELAND'S REVOLT IN '98.

CHAPTER I.

AGITATION PRECEDING THE REBELLION.

Among the venerable storytellers to whom the youth of our native village looked for information about those past troubled times—the gloomiest in Ireland's records—the writer recalls one whose gray hairs and well-known intelligence made him listened to with respect by old and young. He was past seventy years, and his memory went back with great clearness to all the minute details of the rebellion.

No wonder he remembered it. At the outbreak he was in his twentieth year; was himself arrested and locked up a prisoner in the market-house of a neighboring town, among a crowd of other rebels, for a whole day, expecting to be hanged, as scores of his companions met their fate before his eyes. Often he pointed out to us the place where the scaffold was erected. Many a brave life was here sacrificed in the cause of freedom! Fortunately he had a friend among the yeomanry, in whose hands the fate of all the prisoners lay, and by special pleading he was liberated at the last moment. "I never felt death so near," he would say, "as I did on that day."

His place of residence throughout the whole of his long life was close to the leading highway in the centre of the village. On fine days he could be seen regularly seated on a wooden bench placed near the door porch, where he could see all who passed on their way to the fair or market.. Few, indeed, came along whose names he did not know; and all were sure of a hearty word of greeting, as well as some new banter, which put them in the best of humor as they proceeded on their journey. The children who passed daily from school were always attracted by the fresh joke he had prepared for them; and the whole crowd, shouting with merriment, scampered off, eager to repeat at home the friendly remark of the kind old grandfather.

There were three of us schoolmates who, on entering a higher class, were becoming interested in the history of our country, and we talked together about getting a good and full account of the famous rebellion from the lips of the old gentleman, who remembered it all so well.

Felix, being fourteen years old and the senior in our little group, was to be our spokesman, and on a certain afternoon, as we passed our old friend, a request was made that he would give us the desired information.

"With pleasure, my good lads," said he. "Sit here on this bench, all of you, and I will begin at once. But you must know that it will take more than one afternoon to go over the whole story. However, there need be no hurry; you may call every day as you pass from school and I will tell you all in parts.

It may take a whole week before I get to the end."

Tom, who was a younger brother of Felix, and full as anxious to hear new stories, appeared delighted with the cheerful reply given to their request. "I hope," said he, "it will not fatigue you to repeat so many things. I think we will have many questions to ask."

"Don't fear for that," answered the kind old man. "I like to see young people seeking information about the past history of their country and I am never tired going over those scenes now long passed, and recalling those persons who were famous in my younger days."

"To begin, I must remind you that the actual rebellion did not last long. The first conflict took place on the 23d day of May, and all was over about the middle of November. It was a contest of not more than six months' duration. Preparations had been going on secretly for some time. There was a good deal of agitation, among those who had the courage to speak, for the previous seven years. The active organization of the revolt was hardly begun two years before.

Indeed, ever since the American colonies cast off the yoke of England, twenty-two years just passed, and established themselves as the United States—a free and independent republic, the people of Ireland began to take courage. Before that happy event Ireland had been for a good while completely disheartenced. The revolution in France, also in the year 1789, roused a new spirit of hope throughout Ireland, as well as every other nation struggling for independence. The public press became bolder in its censures of the corrupt methods of government then prevalent. Several clever writers among the patriots had printed, both in newspapers and pamphlets, severe attacks on the many abuses of those in power. The guilty ones were held up to ridicule in this way in humorous verses and rhymes circulated among the peasantry. Just as you now see those ballad singers in the streets of our towns, so it was then a very general custom to have those patriotic and humorous verses printed and sung at public gatherings. The peasantry of the whole country, who did not have newspapers as we have now, were thus made aware of the state of public affairs.

Public meetings were held, too, as long as the law did not interfere. Stirring speeches were made by educated men, who denounced the many wrongs of the nation, and discussed the various reforms necessary. Those meetings were soon proclaimed unlawful. To take part in them, or to be the author of any printed criticism of the civil administration was punished by heavy fines and imprisonment. These measures drove the people to secret methods of discussing their public grievances. Secret societies were started under various titles. Of these the principal one was that of the "United Irishmen."

The young listeners were all attention as the old man went on. Felix here, with a serious expression on his face, observed: "I suppose there were lots of policemen then, as now, to spy about and report on people." "Not only such as we have now," was the reply, "but there were soldiers stationed in almost every town, who made arrests by order of the nearest magistrate; and there were other spies paid by the government for nothing else but to go about in disguise everywhere and report what they heard and saw."

"Was the rebellion planned by the Catholics?" asked Tom.

"Not at all," replied the grandfather. "It was planned and directed by Protestants from the very beginning, and as long as it lasted. The Catholics were forced into it as the agitation went on, and the great majority of the armed peasantry were Catholics. For a long time they knew they had a just cause for rebellion, and were willing to join in such a movement when they could see a fair prospect of success. They, indeed, had the greatest of reasons for rebelling, as I will explain by and by; but many of them doubted the wisdom of the plans on which it was organized, while others were slow to join because the preparations appeared insufficient.

It may appear strange that they had such earnest friends among their Protestant fellow-countrymen; for the penal laws which so cruelly oppressed them were made by a Protestant government. But it is a fact that the most ardent patriots and rebels were non-Catholics. Many of them were Presbyterians and dissenters of other sects, who had no friendship for the Church of England Protestants. They shared in some of the disabilities that were aimed at Catholics, and thus were led to have sympathy with them in resisting laws that interfered with the religious opinions of both. Besides, in that generation there were great numbers of Protestants of all classes who, although descended from English and Scotch settlers commenced to look upon Ireland as their country, and to take an ardent interest in its welfare. However wrongfully their fathers got hold of their Irish estates, they saw no reason for continuing harsh to their Catholic neighbors who had been robbed of their possessions by unjust laws, and were reduced to a state of misery deplorable enough. They had feelings for those Catholics among whom they were brought up, of whose sufferings they were witnesses, and whose upright and generous character they learned to admire. They had seen their fill of gross persecution for conscience sake from childhood, and were willing to do a service to a people whom their fathers hated and treated as enemies. However they might differ in their religious views, they decided that all could and ought to unite in the removal of political abuses, and in securing for Ireland the ordinary rights of civilized men.

It was a repetition of that spirit which grew up in their kinsmen across the Atlantic twenty-two years before, which led them to unite, without thought of religious differences, and drive forever from American soil the hateful tyranny of a bigoted English aristocracy.

Among the most prominent actors in the insurrection was Theobald Wolf Tone. He was well known to have a dislike for Catholics. The same was said of Grattan, the greatest orator of his time and the tireless advocate of Ireland's rights. Another very upright and disinterested Protestant in the movement was Thomas Addis Emmett."

"Was he the Emmett who was hanged for treason?" asked Tom.

"No," replied the aged historian; "the one to whom you refer was Robert, a brother to Thomas Addis. He was hanged for planning another insurrection a few years afterwards."

"As the society called 'United Irishmen' was the organization that gave birth to the insurrection at this time, we do well to recall in a few words its early movements. It was founded in Belfast in the year 1791 by a party of twenty young patriotic citizens. The leading and most active member was Wolf Tone, now in his twenty-eighth year. He was a native of Kildare, a prominent lawyer, and popular agitator. Through him a branch was soon formed in Dublin; and from these two centres it spread to all parts of the country. The first object thought of was a reform of parliament."

"What was wrong with parliament that they wanted reformed?" said Felix. "You are right in asking that question, my boy," answered the grandfather. "To know that will help us to understand the cause of so much discontent and murmurs among the people for many years before as well as since." An honest parliament would be formed of members elected by the people of the country, and would pay attention to the interests of the people who elected them. But the Irish parliament was never an honest one. The members were seldom of the people's choice. The great majority of them got their places by sham elections, by bribery, or by influence of friends who forced voters by threats of various kinds. Instead of being the choice of the people, they were the favorites of the rich foreign landlords.

"I suppose," said Tom, "the voters were led to the polls as we saw the crowd of tenants last week following their landlord between two lines of soldiers to take care of them as they trotted along like a flock of sheep."

"Just so," was the reply. "That was one way of doing it, quite common then. Such ridiculous sights got to be so common that the shame of it was not felt by the so-called 'gentry' who owned the land and the people who cultivated it, as if they were of no account except to produce a revenue for their masters. But worse still: the Catholics, who were the great majority of the population, were not allowed to vote at all; even when holding land as tenants, while to aspire to be a member of parliament was expressly forbidden to them in one of the penal laws.

The oath taken by the new society called 'United Irishmen' was 'to forward a brotherhood of affection, an identity of interests, a communion of rights, and a union of power among Irishmen of all denominations.'

Their efforts were to be directed to procuring honest and free elections for all future members of parliament; and put an end to the old practice of having strangers forced upon them against their will, every denomination being fairly represented in both houses of legislature.

In Dublin the regular meeting place chosen by the society was a spacious building called Tailors' Hall, in Back Lane. From the number of popular gatherings held here it was commonly called the 'Back Lane Parliament.'

At this famous hall many fervid speeches were made by such noted members as Simon Butler, a barrister; by Napper Tandy, a merchant of the city, and by Oliver Bond. Among the Catholics who regularly attended were John Keogh and McCormick.

As might be expected, there were spies sent by the Castle to watch all the proceedings. The meetings were declared illegal, and several arrests followed, on the charge of having used seditious language and censured the ruling powers.

The society was forced now to conduct its deliberations in secret. The abuses in parliament were beyond all hope of correction. That body had become a rotten thing, unworthy of the name, and deserved to be blotted out of existence. Complete separation from English rule was resolved upon as the only possible remedy, and a republic for Ireland was planned after that lately established in France.

The arming of the whole population secretly was devised, as well as a method of calling them to action when the time should seem ripe, and take possession of all the strongholds in the hands of the royal troops.

The aid of France and any other friendly power was to be secured, and agents were dispatched to settle such alliances as early as it could be accomplished.

The revolutionary movements of this armed population in every part of the country were directed by a committee of five members with supreme authority, called the 'Executive Directory.' This was located in Dublin. Each of the provinces had its directory, under control of that at headquarters. Each county had its committee to attend to the enrolment of the local organizations. A careful system of transmitting orders from the supreme lodge through all the different degrees down to the common ranks was contrived, to keep the plans secret from all not in sympathy with the rebels.

CHAPTER II.

CAUSES OF DISCONTENT.

On the following day, as our young schoolmates walked together on their way home, they discussed several matters that were not quite clear to them in the course of Irish affairs, and they decided to ask an explanation at their next meeting with their aged historian. One thing they wished to learn was the meaning of the penal laws.

Glad to see their growing interest in such important points in their country's history, he assented, and, clearing his throat, he began, as follows: "Your question is quite natural. I will give you a full list of those inhuman laws in a future conversation. It would delay my story too much to explain all of them now. But a few of the worst which caused such terrible wrong and discontent among the people may be noticed before I go farther. The penal laws were contrived to force Catholics to adopt the Protestant Church of England, or, in case they refused and yet remained in the country, to deprive them of the right to vote or to hold any office under government—to deprive them of education, and gradually take out of their hands all property, whilst they were to be repeatedly fined and imprisoned for neglecting to attend the Protestant form of worship.

"How these laws worked in reducing the Catholic people to a state of poverty and dependence we have plenty of evidence before our eyes. During those long years of oppression there were a few here and there to give up their religion in order to keep their property in their hands and to get the education that was offered to them on such base terms. But perverts of this kind were very few, indeed, compared with the great body of the nation who, holding to their faith, were driven to beggary and a condition no better than slavery in their native land.

"These laws were repealed some years ago through the agitation of the great O'Connell. I attended some meetings where he spoke on that subject. I was a young man then; and I tell you he could rouse the people to the highest pitch of enthusiasm by his eloquence. At meetings held all over the country he called the attention of the whole world to the meanness of these laws, and when reasoning did no good he shamed the government into granting the repeal.

"You are lucky, my boys, to have your good schools so near you. If you lived in those times you would have no chance to learn to read or write unless you became little Protestants; which I am sure you never would do. Things are improving slowly. But we have not well recovered from the effects of those laws yet."

"Another thing that Tom wanted to ask

about," said Felix, "is the meaning of what they call tithes."

"Well," said the old man, "that was another wretched business that caused no end of trouble."

"Tithes were a tax forced from the people for the support of Protestant clergymen placed by English government in charge of churches scattered all over the country. Even in localities where no Protestants lived there were parishes formed and churches built at the expense of Catholic taxpayers."

"I suppose," said Tom, "like the small church yonder near Landlord Hopkins's big house. They say that the minister has none to preach to except his wife and children, and the sexton, and the landlord, when he is at home."

"In many places," said the grandfather, "such was the case." "Now, Tom, just imagine one of those visitors calling at your father's house some fine morning to demand the tithes for his support. It was a common practice for many years. Along with the minister would come the sheriff and several soldiers from the nearest barracks—all on horseback. The amount they must get was fixed beforehand. Your property was valued—that is, your cattle, your crops, and all about your house. Their part was to be the tenth, or as near it as they could get, every year. If you refused to pay it they could drive off a part of your cattle; and if you had no cattle, they would take some of the furniture, or clothing —perhaps your mother's best dress—anything that could be auctioned off to get the amount of cash you were supposed to owe for the support of the minister and his family.

Another hardship that goaded the people to have recourse to arms was the free quartering of the royal troops in the homes of the suspected inhabitants. Soldiers were billeted among the people of all classes, so that every family had to give free lodging and board to one or more of those disgusting redcoats. I don't think, Tom, you would like to see one of those greedy and lazy orange soldiers settling himself in your father's house, taking the best room to sleep in, and demanding the best food in the place. Your mother's fattest chickens would soon be eaten up, and when the fowl were all gone the big appetites of these brutish fellows would have to be appeased by some other meat, even if the best cow on the farm was to be killed for that purpose."

"I would shoot him," said the young lad, as his face grew red and a fierce expression brightened his eyes.

"It would not be easy to do it," continued the old man. "The people all felt like you; but it would be useless to attack such well-armed lodgers. It was, indeed, impossible to have patience at times; and many a fearful encounter arose between the master of the house and the brutish, saucy lodger.

As it was the most barbarous of all the late acts of government, so it was the surest way that could be tried to excite the people to frenzy, and force them to take up arms, even though death stared them in the face."

CHAPTER III.

EFFORTS TO SECURE FOREIGN AID.

"Now we must return to where we left off," commenced the grandfather, when his young listeners took their places on the bench beside him for the third time. "The patriots, you will recollect, decided to apply to some foreign nation to assist them. Of course France was the first to come to their minds, as its people had been always friendly to Ireland and had kept up the old warlike feeling against England.

Wolf Tone offered himself for the important mission. He was obliged to fly at this time from the danger of arrest which threatened him, and he succeeded in eluding the officers sent on his track. On a vessel bound for the United States he got off safely, determined to reach France on another ship starting from some American port, and, perhaps, gain some sympathy and assistance in negotiating the business he had in hands.

In this he was not disappointed. His enthusiasm in the cause of liberty for his country must have grown still greater on this visit to a new people already enjoying the blessings of independence. There were many Irishmen there who had fought well in the American war to drive England from that country for

IRELAND'S REVOLT IN '98

ever; and they were glad to hear from him any prospects of gaining the same freedom for Ireland.

When starting from New York he was suplied with letters of introduction to prominent politicians in France who could help him in carrying out his projects. One of these was the American ambassador at Paris, Mr. Monroe, who afterwards became president of the United States.

Arrived in Paris in February, 1796, he was received with favor, and everything promised well for the cause. Among the distinguished officers then at the head of the French army were Napoleon, Hochè and Grouchy. They took an active part in forwarding Tone's object.

After some delay a fleet was got ready consisting of 17 sail of the line, 13 frigates and 13 smaller ships carrying 15,000 picked troops. It started from Brest, December 16th, '96. Tone accompanied the expedition, holding the rank of Colonel on the staff of General Hochè.

The fleet reached the coast of Ireland after three days' sail without encountering any English ships in the passage. After entering Bantry Bay on the coast of Kerry a landing of the troops was decided upon. The day happened to be the Feast of Christmas. A violent storm, however, arising in the night before the time set for debarkation the ships were forced to stand out far from shore; and after waiting some days for favorable weather it was decided to put off the invasion and return to France.

While Tone was thus occupied with the French another agent from Ireland was sent to Holland, now a new Republic under the name of Batavia. The agent's name was Lewines. He was successful also as well as Tone in securing a fleet to act in union with that of France.

Fine promises, at least, were made; and a fleet fitted out ready to embark. But one delay after another followed—chiefly on account of unfavorable weather, and at last the troops were ordered ashore with no hope of resuming the project.

Wolf Tone in the face of these disappointments was not to be discouraged. Again he busied himself among the French allies, and soon a third expedition was got ready which he accompanied in the rank of adjutant-general in the Fall of '98; but of this I will say more later on."

Felix could hardly keep Tom quiet in his eagerness to ask some new question that came to his mind during the latter part of the story.

"We must not interrupt the conversation," he often whispered to his young companion. It was agreed, however, between them that the next day they would inquire what was going on in Ireland while Tone was absent in France.

"Very well," said the old man, when the matter was brought up at their next meeting. "I am ready now to tell you all about that."

"The patriots at home were not idle during

all this time. The men of greatest ability and prominence at the head of the movement in Dublin where the Directory kept its office were Thomas Russell, Thomas Addis Emmet, Arthur O'Connor, and Dr. McNevin.

The work of enrolling the peasantry throughout Ireland as members of the United Irishmen went on steadily. Towards the close of the year '97 there were 500,000 reported ready to take up arms when called upon. Of these about 300,000 had secured firelocks or pikes; 100,000 belonged to Ulster; about 60,000 were counted from Leinster, and the remainder from Connaught and Munster.

The office of Commander-in-chief was given to Lord Edward Fitzgerald, a young and active patriot who had been formerly a Major in the British army.

For all these recruits there was not a supply of arms and other necessary stores; but for such supplies they depended on France; and they delayed the time of rising until the arrival of the fleet expected through the exertions of Wolfe Tone.

Although these plans were laid with the greatest secrecy you will not wonder to hear that the castle officials at Dublin were informed of everything by their spies, who carried the news to them from day to day.

Several arrests were made. The most active leaders were cast into prison. I am sorry to have to say that there were some traitors among the rebels who reported to the authorities at the Castle all that was going on. For this, of course, they were well rewarded; for bribes were held out every day to any such mean wretches who would betray their countrymen.

It may appear strange to you when I say that the English government desired to see the Irish start a rebellion. Although there was a good deal of show made of opposition to an insurrection, yet all this time and for some years before the officials of the castle tried various ways of provoking the people to open warfare.

Here Felix spoke up. "Do you mean," said he, "that the English wished the Irish to rebel—forced them to rebel, and then arrested them and hanged them for rebelling?"

"Exactly," was the reply.

"I would be a rebel, too!" shouted Tom excitedly, "if I lived in those times!"

"That is what a great, honest English soldier, Sir John Moore, said when he saw how the Irish were treated," replied the grandfather. His words were: "If I were an Irishman I would be a rebel. "

"The reason why the English government were pleased to see an Irish insurrection break out was in order to have a pretext for doing away with the Irish parliament, and uniting Ireland with England to be ruled only by the English parliament in London.

All this was planned by the ministers of George III. even as early as '93. The Irish parliament had become a tool in the hands of those ministers who were sent over year after year to create new members of the House of Lords such as would be ready to vote any measure the King's deputies wanted, and to fill the House of Commons with a crowd of members not by honest elections, but by bribery and other disreputable methods.

In such a parliament it was easy to rush through those various oppressive laws which followed.

The Catholics were deprived of all voice at elections. It was declared unlawful for anyone to have arms in his possession. A new power was given to common magistrates everywhere, and even to military officers, to arrest and convict anyone they might suspect as favoring the rebelion.

The English troops stationed in the various districts could do as they pleased. These soldiers cared nothing for the feelings of the families where they took forcible lodging. They were Orangemen for the most part; and, of course, it was their inclination to be as insulting as possible to the Catholics whilst it was their business to provoke resistance.

You easily see that where common soldiers were allowed such liberties the life of a rebel, or one suspected as a rebel, was not thought of much value.

Wherever the officers happened to be unusually cruel and brutish many innocent persons were executed without the formality of a trial, and various kinds of cruelties were inflicted on the defenseless peasantry—sometimes to terrify them into submission and sometimes to extort information about those suspected of disloyalty. Some of these cruelties make one shudder to think of them. It is only among savage nations we could imagine such horrors possible.

The testimony of a new commander of the royal forces sent over in November, '97, leaves no doubt on the subject. He was a gallant Scotch soldier with half a century of brave service in his record, and after a week's residence in Dublin he was forced to condemn in the most energetic terms the barbarous policy of government as administered at that time. Writing in confidence to his son, he says: "The abuses of all kinds I found here can scarcely be believed or enumerated."

CHAPTER IV.
CONFLICT BEGUN.

No wonder that the rising was hastened under such a state of things. Although favorable reports continued to come from Tone and his companions in France yet it was thought better delay the actual uprising until the expected troops and supplies should land.

The government forces were now increased at the different garrisons throughout the provinces. Of yeomanry—chiefly Orangemen and militia with English and Scotch corps there were about 35,000. Of regular troops with new additions the number was 80,000.

Against this army of 115,000 men the rebels could count on 300,000 ready to take the field, but, of course, not so well armed and without the training and discipline of regular troops.

The Castle authorities at Dublin became alarmed on learning that the city garrisons were to be among the first marked out for an attack.

During the first months of '98 important arrests were made among the heads of the insurrection. Among them were Father James Quigley, Arthur O'Connor and the brothers John and Benjamin Binn. They were intercepted on their way to France towards the end of February. On the 12th of March the Leins-

C

ter delegates were seized with all their papers at the house of Oliver Bond in Bridge street, Dublin. Thomas Addis Emmet and Dr. McNevin were taken in their own houses, and William Sampson in the north of England. Lord Edward Fitzgerald, the commander-in-chief of the rebel army, after evading the government spies successfully for two months, was at last taken on the 19th of May at his hiding place in Thomas street.

Left without a head, the insurgents determined to go on and strike the first blow on the 23d, as had been decided some time before.

The signal for making the first attack was the departure of the mail coaches from the Dublin post office at night. They were to be simultaneously stopped.

The assault to be made on the castle and other forts about the city had to be abandoned; but a well armed force of insurgents commenced action at Rathfarnham, a village about three miles northwest of the city, where a body of yeomanry under Lord Ely were stationed. The charge was successful for some time and a retreat made only after a force of dragoons under Lord Roden arrived in haste from the city.

The garrison at Naas, in Kildare County, was also attacked by a large force. Three times the charge was made with great determination, but the rebels were forced to yield after losing 140 of their men.

Similar engagements took place at no less

than a dozen places in the one county of Kildare. Never did soldiers fight with more resolution, as never did a people rise in self-defence having a more just cause for going to war. But something else was needed as well as heroism and courage. The want of effective arms alone prevented success. The old-fashioned pikes and firelocks could aid little in resisting the charge of cavalry and an unfailing supply of ammunition.

At the town of Prosperous a small garrison of Cork militia was cut off by a brave charge under Dr. Esmonde. This brave leader was betrayed a few weeks afterward and executed.

At Monasterevan the rebels were repulsed with great loss. They were victors at Rathanagan, where they held the town for several days. The force that captured Prosperous tried to repeat their skill of arms in Clane, but were forced to retire.

At old Kilcullen a strong force of the regular army was defeated, having lost 22 men along with Captian Erskine.

In one week from the first battle the Kildare fighting was all over. The six encampments of rebels in this county were dispersed, and all their most active officers were in prison or had fled to the south or west.

An important movement was planned by several adjoining counties. Their united forces were to meet on the famous hill of Tara on the 27th of May in order to make a bold attack on some neighboring posts of the enemy.

The men of Cavan, Longford, Louth and Monaghan were late in arriving on the date fixed, and a powerful government force reached the place before them and surrounded the hill. The rebel camp, however, small as it was, made a desperate fight in defending their position, and, although forced to retire, they left 26 Highlanders and six yeomanry dead on the field.

At Dunlavin an attack on the barracks failed. During the engagement here it turned out that some of the yeomanry were in sympathy with the rebels. By order of a military inquiry into their guilt 19 Wexfordmen and 9 Kildare men were executed.

Next followed assaults on the towns of Blessington and Carlow. The former was besieged and easily taken; at the latter the enemy proved too strong.

We now turn to Wexford where the fiercest fighting took place. In no other part of Ireland did the royal troops meet such long and stubborn resistance. Although this county was not reported as having made much preparation for the revolt it turned out soon to be the best united when the spark of war was fanned by the news from other conflicts.

The people of this section were rather opposed to the rising as it had been planned; for they adopted the opinion of the Catholic clergy generally that the country was not sufficiently prepared for such a vast undertaking when the strength of the English forces now increased at all points was considered.

But after the actual conflict when tidings of partial victories on the side of the insurgents spread as far as the Southern provinces the natives became more hopeful and emboldened to take a part along with their brethren of the central and northern counties.

Besides the conduct of the troops of yeomanry at the different garrisons became more and more brutal. Groundless charges against the peaceful inhabitants were everywhere made. Outrages of the most barbarous kind were inflicted on people on the mere suspicion of disloyalty; and so intense were the feelings of resentment roused in the breasts of all that it became impossible to restrain them any longer. From peaceful citizens they were driven to the desperate resolution of defending by arms what they despaired of saving by peaceful measures.

We notice here a rather singular feature in the uprising not found in other places. It is the active part taken by several priests in some important battles.

The young listeners showed more and more eagerness to catch every word as the story grew full of new and startling events.

"I thought," broke in Felix, "that priests could not take part in war."

"They are not allowed by the rules of the church to carry arms or fight in battle," replied the grandfather. "In case a priest's life is threatened he can lawfully defend himself like any other man. But beyond that priests are not to take part in the shedding of blood. On the battlefield they are allowed to be present for the purpose of giving spiritual aid to the dying, and in this way they bear a very valuable part in every just war.

At this particular time in Wexford there were circumstances which appeared to justify the unusual part which they did take.

Among the many atrocities inflicted on the quiet peasantry by the insulting royal troops was the burning of the Catholic chapels throughout the country. There were 65 of these houses of worship destroyed in Leinster alone during the rebellion, and 22 of them belonged to Wexford. It is worth notice that only one Protestant church was destroyed in retaliation during the same period.

The names of the priests who led the rebels in battle were Father John Murphy of Kilcormick, Father Michael Murphy of Gorey, Father Philip Roche, Father Clinch and Father Kearns.

One fine morning—it was Whit Sunday, May 27th—as Father John Murphy visited his chapel at Kilcormick he found the building in ashes—the work of a body of yeomanry who had passed that way.

His indignation was aroused. From that moment his mind was made up to lead his people in defence of their homes and lives now exposed every momnt to the license of the foreign troops. He addressed the congregation assembled around him, and in view of the ruined chapel he offered himself to be their leader even in armed resistance, since there was now no other way of removing the horrors from which they suffered. Was it not better, he said, to meet death in a fair field than suffer the tortures which they could hardly escape in their peaceful homes.

In a short time 2,000 of the country people were under his command. A supply of arms was hastily collected and every man prepared to do his part, making up by enthusiasm and valor for the imperfect manner of their equipment. This sturdy band took a position on the hill called Oulart, about 11 miles north of the town of Wexford, where they hoped to be joined soon by a much larger force. They were attacked on the same afternoon by the royalist troops, composed of North Cork militia under Colonel Foote, with some yeomen and Wexford cavalry.

Aided by their position the rebels made a brave defence. They proved themselves skilled in the use of arms. The attacking troops began to fall fast from the moment they came within sight, and leaving their dead and wounded scattered around the base of the hill the cavalry turned back, galloping in disorder to the county town.

The success of this beginning was reported quickly all over the county, and the people became thoroughly aroused.

On the same day Father Michael Murphy, who was parish priest of Gorey, found his chapel wrecked, and like his brother John at Kilcormick, full of indignation, he proceeded at once to join the rebels, who were assembled at Kilthomas Hill, near Carnew. Means were taken to notify every section of the county to unite in arms. Bonfires were kindled on the tops of the highest hills as signals to the inhabitants, while horsemen were dispatched to give orders everywhere as the leaders had decided.

The insurgents found themselves strong enough to seize the neighboring towns held by the royal troops.

On the 28th they took possession of Ferns, Camolin and Enniscorthy after a short encounter. In taking the latter town the fight lasted four hours, when the yeomanry lost 80 men, a captain, and two lieutenants. The rest fled to Wexford, where was stationed a strong garrison, composed of 300 North Cork militia, 200 Donegal, and 700 of the home militia. Here the town was surrendered to the rebels without opposition.

On the 30th of the month (Wednesday) a large force of the enemy from the fortress at Duncannon advanced to retake the town; but they were attacked unexpectedly from the rebel camp that had prepared for the assault a few miles outside the town. The enemy lost three officers and about 100 men. Besides the number killed there were several prisoners as well as three howitzers and 11 gunners seized by the rebels. Those three considerable victories inside of one week inspired the victors with greater ambition. They naturally believed the northern and midland counties equally active ,or, at least able to keep in check the royalist forces in their province; and a determination was formed to march on even as far as Dublin itself.

With this object the main part of their body was to advance under command of Anthony Perry, Esmond Kyan and the two brother priests, Fathers John and Michael Murphy. Their route for the capital was to take in the towns of Arklow and Wicklow.

A second division under Father Kearns and Father Clinch, as well as Messrs. Fitzgerald, Doyle and Redmond, was to attack New Ross, and endeavor to hasten the rising in Munster.

A third division led by Father Philip Roche and Bagnal Harvey planned a union with Carlow, Kilkenny and Kildare.

The first division proceeded northward on the 1st of June with the object of capturing Gorey. This town contained a strong force of the enemy under General Loftus. The rebels were met by a detachment sent out to meet them. In an encounter following they were defeated and driven back with a loss of 100 killed and wounded.

Re-enforcements now arriving from various quarters to aid the enemy, a united attack was planned under Loftus, by which the rebel camp on Corrigrua Hill would be forced to surrender. This design was foreseen by the rebels, and they made their own arrangements.

A position was taken along the main road leading to their former elevated fortifications on the hill. Convinced that the enemy would surely pass that way in full force they concealed themselves among the thick growth of shrubbery that grew on either side where the road bends through a narrow valley with deep trenches and uneven mounds of earth, offering a secure retreat.

The enemy advancing with solid ranks fell into the trap prepared for them, and unsuspecting anything to impede their progress a sudden volley from the rebel ambush fell among the troops with deadly effect.

The first fire was followed up by a general charge from the rebels, who rushed from their hiding places and completely overpowered the unsuspecting troops.

The desperate charge was continued all along the line. Colonel Walpole fell among the first, and hundreds of the common ranks lay strewn along the highway. Three guns were captured—two six-pounders and one howitzer—and used against the routed royalists, who were now in utter confusion and put to flight. A supply of ammunition and other valuable spoils were taken.

Meanwhile the body of rebels under Fathers Kearns and Clinch left their camping ground on Vinegar Hill and prepared for the siege of Newtownbarry. The royalist garrison here was under command of Colonel L'Estrange, and amounted to about 800 regulars with a troop of dragoons and supplied with two battalion guns.

On the 2d of June the assault was commenced. The rebels took possession after a short but lively conflict. Their success, however, they neglected to follow up. Precious time was lost while they dispersed for plunder or refreshment; and the enemy rallying for a fresh encounter, re-entered the town in triumph. In this action the rebels lost 400 of their men.

CHAPTER V.

BATTLES AT NEW ROSS, ARKLOW, AND VINEGAR HILL.

Decisive engagements now followed in rapid succession. That at New Ross is the next to deserve notice. The leaders of the insurgents in this action were Father Roche and Bagenal Harvey. The force at their command was considerable. Some reported it as 20,000 men. This is probably an exaggeration.

However, the town was well fortified and presented difficulties rather serious even to this large invading army.

On the 5th of June the conflict began. For 10 hours the besieged resisted the determined charge of the rebels, who at last entered the town as victors. The garrison lost one colonel, three captains, and 200 among the ranks. The loss on the other side was three times that number.

The victory here, however, was spoiled in the same way as at Newtownbarry three days before. Needing rest and refreshment after the prolonged encounter of the forenoon the rebels gave an opportunity to the enemy to rally their forces and return conquerors into the town from which they had been lately expelled.

The insurgents retired in security to their camp on Corbet Hill.

The rebel division that we left victorious at Gorey decided to march on Arklow. With this object they set out on the 9th of June. As the town was situated on the coast it had received new supplies recently from the English fleet that had been cruising in the channel for some time.

From Dublin also came additional forces to its defence under General Needham. The attack was expected and a strong barricade was constructed on all the main approaches. Yet there was nothing in all this to lessen the ardor of the rebels to continue their successful course.

The enemy, however, had so many advantages on their side that bravery and numbers could not make up for discipline.

After an engagement that lasted six hours the rebels lost 1,500 of their men and were forced to retreat, taking with them a large number of wounded. The royalists acknowledged the loss of 100 killed, including Captain Knox, and about as many wounded.

In this battle Father Michael Murphy fell after bravely leading his men to the charge for the third time.

The scattered rebels were now obliged to unite their forces on Vinegar Hill to be able to resist the combined armies that arrived from different quarters with the intention of striking a decisive blow at the rebellion in that county.

The prospects had become less hopeful now for them. Munster had still remained inactive, while the North and West did not engage the attention of the new re-enforcements from England.

Vinegar Hill, therefore, was to be the battlefield for all Wexford, and a united effort was to be made against such an overwhelming force.

Lord Lake had charge of the royalists as commander-in-chief. His attack on the rebel encampment was fixed for the 20th of June. All his available forces were ordered to take up commanding positions under six generals, as follows: General Dundas arriving from Wicklow, was to join Loftus at Carnew; Henry Johnson, with Sir James Duff at Old Ross; Sir Charles Asgill was to occupy Gore's bridge and Borris. Sir John Moore was to join his forces lately landed with Johnson and Duff.

Part of these arrangements were prevented by unexpected encounters with rebel detachments, but on the appointed day the royal troops drawn about the hill were altogether about 13,000. The rebel camp contained 20,-000. The different columns of the enemy advanced up the slopes of the hill on three sides and opened a steady fire on the rebels.

They met with a desperate resistance, which was kept up for an hour and a half. At length the contest proved unequal. The deadly effect of the enemy's guns on different points produced a panic. The rebels broke into a disorderly flight by the unguarded side of the hill. Pursued by the royalist cavalry over the level country they were cut down without resistance and lost during the encounter not less than 400 of their number.

The loss on the other side was about 200 killed and wounded. The only leader among the rebels to fall here was Father Clinch. During the retreat he encountered Lord Roden, whom he wounded, but was himself shot down by a trooper who came to the rescue of his general.

After this defeat the insurgents dispersed in several distinct bands; some by way of Gorey towards the Wicklow mountains; others retiring nearer the coast, or wherever they could await in security for new tidings from their confederates of Munster, whom they long expected to come forward to their aid.

The town of Wexford surrendered to Lord Lake on the 22d, and Father Roche, with Harvey, his fellow leader, having lost all hope, laid down their arms. Although their surrender was accepted with the condition of clemency they were executed soon after along with many others who yielded to the victors on what they understood to be honorable terms.

Of the engagements immediately following in this province there were two quite notable and of serious embarrassment to the royal troops.

One took place in Wicklow and the other at Castlecomer, in the County of Kilkenny.

The insurgents in the County Wicklow were not as strong in numbers as their neghbors of Wexford, but they were able to hold in check the advances of the king's army much longer on account of the character of the country.

Deep glens and a variety of mountain retreats which abound everywhere furnished them with valuable posts of defence.

They were not wanting in vigorous preparation when the news spread from other scenes of battle.

Their most noted leaders were the Byrne brothers of Ballymanus, with their able comrades, Holt and Hackett.

On the 25th of June a brief engagement took place at Hacketstown that turned out against them, but on the 30th they obtained a decided victory at Ballyellis, where they were attacked by a stong detachment under General Needham.

A trap was laid for the enemy similar to that near the town of Wexford some days before and was equally successful. Needham's army was decoyed into a ravine, where a skilful ambuscade was set for them by the rebels, who fell upon them with a deadly fire. Two officers were killed along with 60 of the rank. The rest fled in disorder to the shelter of their camp. Other skirmshes of a similar kind took place on the 2d of July, but on the 4th the insurgents were surrounded by various detachments of the enemy and forced to surrender.

Father Kearns, with Anthony Perry, who

had taken part in the battle at Vinegar Hill, marched into Kildare to join some confederate bands still remaining armed in that section. After a futile attempt to reach Athlone they were forced to seek for safety by dispersing in small bodies, and the brave leaders, Father Kearns and Mr. Perry were taken prisoners and executed.

Another band of Wexford men led by Father John Murphy and Walter Devereux, after the Vinegar Hill defeat, proceeded to the adjoining County of Kilkenny. They besieged Castlecomer and easily took possession of the town. After this they advanced toward Athy in Kildare. Several divisions of the government troops from the neighboring garrisons here stopped their progress, and they returned to Old Leighlin. Father Murphy was captured and conveyed a pisoner to General Duff's headquarters at Tullow. He was tried by a military commission and convicted as a very dangerous rebel was executed. His body was burned and his head spiked on the market house of Tullow.

CHAPTER VI.

SOME BATTLES IN ULSTER.

Friends of the revolution had looked to Ulster for great things from the beginning. It was there that the patriotic spirit first burst out, and plans were laid five years before the actual outbreak. In no other province were the people so well organized. The counties of Antrim and Down were especially active. A determined effort was in preparation until the chief leaders, Thomas Russell and Samuel Neilson were imprisoned. A delay of some weeks was caused by several unexpected movements on the part of the government, which now seemed to be aware of everything planned in the rebel camps.

It was decided to capture the town of Antrim first as a most favorable centre of operations, this point being of easy access to the different organizations in Donegal and Down.

In the absence of the original leaders a prominent Belfast cotton manufacturer named McCracken volunteered to assume command. On the 7th of June the assault was made. Victory was on the side of the rebels, and they were on the point of entering the town when a detachment of the royal forces arrived to aid their besieged brethren, and compelled the assailants to retreat. In this battle about 300 of the rebels fell. Of the besieged there were five officers and forty-seven of the rank among the killed. Some weeks later Mr. McCracken and his staff were arrested and after a trial at Belfast were executed.

On the same day while the battle was fought at Antrim another engagement took place at Saintfield in the County Down, where the rebel force was led by Dr. Jackson. The army on the other side was under Colonel Stapleton and had to retreat with loss. On the 13th Ballinahinch was the scene of a conflict between the insurgents under Henry Munro and the regular government troops led by General Nugent. The battle raged with desperation on the part of the rebels, who held out with great energy; but they were finally defeated. Munro, their leader, was captured two days after the battle and was executed at his own home in Lisburn.

The actual warfare in the province continued only one week. In Munster there was hardly any attempt at insurrection during all this time. Only one skirmish occurred near the town of Bandon between some imperfectly armed peasantry and the Westmeath yeomanry. Neither side claimed any material advantage.

CHAPTER VII.

AID FROM FRANCE ARRIVES.

As the aged narrator went on describing these stormy events he was listened to attentively by the young inquirers.

At length they thought a question might be asked here without interrupting the course of the story.

"Grandfather," said Felix, "did not the French arrive yet to help at the right time?"

"Not yet," was the reply. "They were anxiously looked for since the beginning of May. Three months had now passed without any tidings from those expected allies. They were three months of almost incessant warfare, during which the native insurgents were left to their own resources. If assistance had come at the appointed time they would certainly have driven the whole English army out of Ireland."

Here Tom, the youngest of the listeners, thought he might venture to express his opinion.

"I am afraid," said he, with an anxious expression on his face, "their guns were not of the best make."

"Indeed they were far from being in good condition," was the reply. "They were of the old pattern in use at that time, and, of course, we must expect that streaks of rust were very common on the best of them. Besides, the greater part of those peasant soldiers so hasily taken from their ploughs and domestic occupations, had no guns at all, but did their fighting with these rude weapons of the country called pikes."

"Pray tell us, grandfather," rejoined Tom, what sort of weapon was the pike?"

"It was somewhat similar to a spear in shape and size," replied the aged historian. A stout wooden pole finished at the end with an iron blade of keen edge and wicked looking point— that was the sort of battle ax which did such damage to the ranks of the English regulars in the hands of our Irish recruits. Of artillery equipment, such as cannon and other heavy engines of war, the supply was very small. A limited number of such guns had been secretly brought over from the continent, and a few more were captured from the King's regiments at various successful raids by the rebels. This short supply was of little use against an enemy so numerous and completely armed.

To resume the course of events after the Ulster campaign at Ballinahinch our attention is called to Connaught.

This province was well organized from an early date. Several thousand refugees who had fled here from the North during the Orange oppression of '95, '96 and '97 taught the Western people the necessity and the art of armed resistance.

On the 22d of August the much desired news of a French fleet appearing off the coast of Sligo spread delight among the native patriots. Three frigates anchored in Kilala Bay with 1,000 men and a supply of arms for a like number, as well as other valuable stores, under command of the French General, Humbert.

The arrival of the friendly fleet was inspiring even at this late stage of the conflict. It was far from being the powerful force promised two years before by the men at the head of affairs then in France.

The neglect to carry out those promises on the part of the French is explained by the unsettled condition of political affairs in the French nation at that time. The new republic had been established only a few years, and complete unity was not yet assured between the leaders having control of government. In such a state of affairs it became possible for General Humbert to fit out this small expedition on his own authority in the absence of Napoleon with his superior forces in the distant Egyptian enterprise.

The French people as a whole were in sympathy with the Irish, and were ready to aid that people in securing independence just as they had so lately helped the Americans to throw off the yoke of England.

But there were jealousies and varied ambitions among the military commanders and others placed in authority, so that the ardent wish of the people, including the great body of the army, was prevented from being fulfilled.

Napoleon sadly regretted afterwards his great mistake in abandoning the Irish at the very moment when everything was favorable for the success of their efforts in the cause of freedom.

In his place of exile at St. Helena he admitted the mistake he had made in not allowing General Hoché to resume the invasion which was commenced at Bantry Bay in the winter of '96. In conversation with Barry O'Meara on this subject he said: "Hoche was one of the first generals France ever produced. He was brave, intelligent, aboundnig in talent, decisive and penetrating. Had he landed in Ireland he would have succeeded. He was accustomed to civil war, had pacified La Vendee, and was well adapted for Ireland. If instead of the expedition to Egypt I had undertaken that to Ireland what could England do now? On such chances depend the destinies of Empires!"

The landing of the French troops and stores at Killala was hastily accomplished. The native leaders of the rebel army in that province were prompt in laying before Humbert their plans of action. The most distinguished among them were Messrs. O'Donnell, Moore, Bellew, Barrett, O'Dowd and O'Donnell of Mayo, Blake of Galway, and Plunket of Roscommon. Three days were spent in distributing arms among the new recruits summoned hastily from every part of the adjoining countics. Part of the time was given to their instruction and drill in the use of arms. The inhabitants of this small seaport town joined heartily in all the bustle and enthusiastic preparation.

Never before in their history did they feel so distinguished or so sure of future glory from the part they were now taking in the cause of their country.

On the fourth day from the landing (Sunday, August 26th) the united forces presented an imposing and formidable column as their solid ranks filed out of the town with banners waving and followed by the loud applause of the inhabitants.

Ballina was the first stronghold to be seized. The town surrendered without resistance, and on the same night the victorious columns marched for Castlebar, the county town. The arrival of the foreign fleet was now known at all the government posts in the country.

Lord Lake and General Hutchinson had already advanced as far as Castlebar, where they had about 3,000 men under their command. Humbert decided to take the enemy by surprise. He had been accustomed to the long marches and difficult country of La Vendee, and a mountain road over the pass of Barnagee offered him a safe route as he descended unexpectedly on the camp of Lake's large army.

On the march the hardy French veterans tramped side by side with the columns of native recruits. The former had been some years inured to the toils of military life in their own revolutionary wars at home, and were equally skilful with the athletic Irish peasants, whether in vaulting over fences that came in their path, or in climbing the steep hillsides, in crossing ravines, or jumping mountain streams.

Their sudden appearance on August 27th in solid, marching columns within view of the enemy's camp caused alarm among Lake's incautious outposts.

Humbert drew up his regiments for immediate action. A prompt and vigorous assault commenced. The enemy repelled the attack with desperate and deadly firing, but after a short conflict were forced into a disorderly retreat They fled in scattered bands—yeomanry and regulars—without stopping until they reached Tuam. Some continued their hasty retreat as far as Athlone, more than 60 miles from the scene of action.

Among the notable incidents of the rebellion this hasty flight has been known as "the races" in the popular language of the country.

Among the officers who distinguished themselves in the battle were Mathew Wolf Tone and Bartholomew Teeling. They accompanied the fleet with Humbert when he set out from La Rochelle. They had been some time in France working with other Irish patriots in the interest of the insurrection.

There was no advantage to be gained by the rebels in continuing the pursuit of the fleeing enemy beyond the limits of the county.

The spoils left in the hands of the victors were of great value. Fourteen British guns and five stand of colors were taken. Of the losses in the ranks on both sides the royalists acknowledged theirs to be as many as 350 men with 18 officers—the French commander estimated the killed on his side to be 600 men.

Although a new body of reinforcements to relieve the royalists appeared on the borders of the County Galway it was decided to avoid a fresh attack until time was taken for deliberation on the campaign to follow.

A provisional government was established at Castlebear, with Mr. Moore, of Moore Hall, as president. Proclamations were addressed to the inhabitants at large; commissions were issued to raise men, and methods adopted to provide for the expenses to be incurred in prosecuting the war.

It was evident that extensive preparations would be needed to make the rebel forces equal to the coming struggle.

Battalions from various British headquarters were advancing toward the camp at Castlebear. Sir John Moore and General Hunter were marching from Wexford towards the Shannon. General Taylor with 2,500 men was on his way to Sligo. Colonel Maxwell was ordered from Enniskillen to assume command at Sligo, while the Viceroy leaving

Dublin in person advanced rapidly through the midland counties to Kilbeggan. Lake and Hutchinson were to muster their scattered regiments and be ready for the assault from headquarters at Tuam.

Humbert found himself now with his whole army, both native and foreign—altogether about 3,000 men—completely hemmed in on every side. His retreat by the sea was also cut off, for the frigates from which he landed had returned to France.

Tidings were brought to him from Ulster and some of the midland counties that several large corps of insurgents were anxious to join him from their various hiding places, and had already started with the hope of effecting a union. Besides, it was understood that another French squadron had set sail and was soon to land on the northern coast. It appeared useless to hazard a battle with the royalist army now massed together in such overwhelming numbers.

Within a short distance opposed to him at least 30,000 well armed troops in several divisions, with as many more in reserve and ready to be called into action at a day's notice.

He decided to advance with all his forces towards Ulster, where the desired relief might come to join him. His route was by the less frequented roads to Coolaney, a distance of 35 miles, which he effected in one day. A corps of the government militia intercepted him here, and turning aside he passed rapidly through Dromahaire, Manorhamilton and Ballintra, making for Granard, where he learned a formidable body of insurgents had made preparations to meet him.

Ever since his landing at Killala several scattered bands of native rebels contrived to muster in considerable force in the counties of Westmeath, Longford, and other counties adjoining. They made heroic efforts to form a junction with the French general and kept him informed of their designs by skilful horsemen who knew all the secluded bypaths and easily evaded the numerous government spies on the way.

When a favorable time arrived this midland force assembled from various quarters and commenced a hasty march to what they hoped to be an important victory for their country. They were formidable in numbers, but their military equipment consisted of a short supply of rifles and the usual home-made pikes. They were doomed to failure, and never meet their French allies. Everything went well on their way through Westmeath, but after passing into the County Longford on the high road approaching the town of Granard a strong body of yeomanry came up and brought them to a halt. A short skirmish took place and ended with a complete victory of the yeomanry. Of the rebels a large number fell by the roadside killed and wounded. When the contest seemed hopeless the greater part fled in different directions, many were taken prisoners and led into the town, where, after a short detention in the market house, they were dragged to the gibbet and the ghastly work of execution went on. The rebels taken in actual warfare were the first victims, but many others of non-combatant peasantry in the neighborhood were arrested on suspicion and met the same fate without the formality of a trial. The horrors here enacted after the battle were never forgotten by the helpless inhabitants. To the present day the most vivid traditions survive of the wholesale butcheries which were witnessed in the public streets.

CHAPTER VIII.

BATTLE OF BALLINAMUCK.

When Humbert reached the eastern borders of Leitrim where it joins the County Longford he decided to pitch his camp at the small village of Ballinamuck. The reinforcements which he sought had not come up, and further progress was hazardous.

On the morning of September 8th, finding himself completely surrounded by the government armies that had got on his track, he prepared to make a last desperate stand. His whole force was only one-tenth of that which he had to face. The conflict was continued for half an hour with deadly effect on both sides. It soon proved useless to prolong the battle.

About 200 of the French having thrown down their arms, the remainder surrendered as prisoners of war. The rebels received no quarter at the hands of the victors. From a field of battle Ballinamuck was turned into a huge slaughter house. While the scaffold was the usual method of execution the bayonet was frequently employed as well as other still more revolting atrocities. Of the leaders Blake, of Galway, was among those executed on the field. A body of Longford and Kilkenny militia, who had joined the rebels, were quickly dispatched. Mr. Moore ended his brief term as president of the Provisional Government by a sentence of banishment. He died on the ship that carried him to exile.

The gallant sons of France in company with Humbert were permitted to travel unarmed to their own country. Forlorn and humiliated on their homeward journey they felt keenly their position and that of their vanquished Irish confederates. They were glad, however, to get off in safety to the shores of a free country, and found some consolation in the prospect of future glory in the military enterprises in which their nation was then engaged.

Ireland's western province now completely overrun by the English battalions, was given up generally to pillage and massacre. All the towns that showed any signs of disloyalty met the vengeance of the conquerers without pity. When Killala was retaken by them the carnage was not confined to rebels in arms. At least 200 of the peaceful inhabitants were put to the sword along with insurgents who offered resistance.

We are accustomed to hear of the bloody and heartless measures perpetrated in France by revolutionists in the wars of La Vendee and Brittany. But the atrocities committed by the royalist army in Ireland during the course of the rebellion surpassed everything before heard of in the armed conflicts of civilized nations.

The candid historian must admit that excesses were committed on both sides. While the conflict raged the fierce passion of revenge led the rebels to acts of cruelty which in our sober judgment we cannot defend and must sincerely regret. Under the circumstances, however, it could hardly be otherwise. A few cases of the kind are recorded in the great Wexford struggle. But it must be borne in mind that the government troops were the first aggressors, that they continued their atrocities for years while the people were noncombatants, and their acts of brutality were not the result of momentary passion, but cool deliberation.

CHAPTER IX.

OTHER EXPEDITIONS FROM FRANCE.

Two additional squadrons bearing French allies to aid the insurgents followed soon after the disaster at Ballinamuck.

On the 17th of September a single brig commanded by General Reay and Napper Tandy reached Rathlin Island, on the coast of Antrim.

Having learned the fate of Humbert these adventurers saw the futility of landing their forces, and without delay returned to the French port, from which they started to await a more favorable chance of success.

On the 20th a new fleet on the same message of friendly aid to Ireland set out from Brest.

It was commanded by Bompart, and consisted of one ship of 74 guns, eight frigates, and two smaller vessels. Three thousand men embarked on board under General Hardi. The indefatigable Theobald Wolfe Tone was among the new invaders holding the rank of adjutant general.

On the 12th of October, after being delayed by storms in the North Atlantic Ocean, the fleet appeared off the coast of Donegal, directing its course towards Lough Swilly. The

E

enemy, however, was close by. An English fleet with an equal number of ships had been cruising on the track of the French, and now came up ready for conflict. On both sides a heavy fire was continued for six hours. The French fought at a disadvantage in commencing without securing their full forces in line. They lost their flagship with two frigates and surrendered. Two more were captured the following day, and the remainder escaped back to France.

CHAPTER X.

FATE OF THE LEADERS.

At the end of the interview in which the foregoing events were recounted by our aged historian the young listeners discussed the subject together on their way home with grave and thoughtful expression in their countenances, and in the very tones of their voice. They suspected that the end of the story was near, and they agreed that an appropriate question to ask next time would be, "What was the fate of the principal leaders of the insurrection."

At their next meeting the old man willingly consented to satisfy their wish and review the names of the most prominent among the patriots with an account of their manner of death or their career after the unsuccessful struggle for freedom. He therefore resumed his story as follows:

"Among the earliest to fall in battle or by the hand of executioners were the gallant Wexfordmen. We will place at the head of the list of popular heroes Edmund Kyan. A few days after the battle of Vinegar Hill he was arrested while secretly paying a visit to his family and instantly put to death. His body was weighted with heavy stones and thrown into Wexford harbor. By favor of the incoming tide a few days after it was deposited on the shore close to the dwelling of his father-in-law, and with friendly care received a Christian burial.

Father Michael Murphy fell in the battle of Arklow on the 9th of June.

Father Clinch met his death at Vinegar Hill, June 20th.

Father Philip Roche, with Bagenal Harvey, and Kelly of Kilane, after surrendering when defeated at Vinegar Hill, were decapitated contrary to the terms agreed to by their victors. Their heads were publicly exposed on iron spikes above the entrance of Wexford Court House for several weeks.

Father Kearns and Anthony Perry were executed by martial law at Edenderry after taking part in the engagement at Kildare in July.

Father John Murphy fell in battle in the County Carlow towards the end of the same month.

Walter Devereux, the colleague of Father Murphy, was arrested in Cork when about to sail for America. He was tried and executed.

Henry John McCracken of Belfast was executed after the battle of Antrim on the 7th of June.

Henry Munro, another sturdy northern leader, was publicly put to death in his own town of Lisburn after the battle of Ballinahinch, June 15th.

Among those who escaped to France, where they afterwards became eminent in various professions were Arthur O'Connor, Corbet, Allen and Ware.

Lord Edward Fitzgerald, who held the post of commander-in-chief of the insurgent army, deserves a more extended notice.

He was a son of the first Duke of Leinster and was born near Dublin, October 15th, 1763. He spent a part of his youth in France, where he pursued a course of studies. After returning to England, and having attained sufficient age, he entered the British army. In the course of the American revolutionary war his regiment was dispatched to take part in that memorable conflict. As aide-de-camp to Lord Rawden he distinguished himself in several engagements. In the latter part of the battle of Eutaw Springs he was severely wounded. When the English forces were defeated and compelled to return home he found an opportunity to enter political life, and became a member of the Irish House of Commons. Subsequently he travelled for some time on the continent, and on his return rejoined his regiment, which was then stationed in Canada.

In 1790 he returned to Ireland. Here he was elected a second time a member of the Irish parliament. In 1792 he visited Paris, where he became associated with the leading revolutionists. While in that city he attended a banquet given by Englishmen, where he publicly renounced his hereditary title, and proposed a toast to the success of the republican arms. Soon after he was dismissed from the British army. He returned to Ireland, where he joined the United Irishmen, of which he was made president in 1796.

Gifted by nature with the qualities which mark the distinguished soldier and popular hero, he readily gained the affection and confidence of the patriots. His valor had been tried in the American campaigns, while his sympathy with the people's aspirations was always candidly expressed. The example of the American heroes valiantly fighting for their independence must have attracted his attention and won his admiration. During the few years spent in France he adopted the republican ideas prevalent in that country. At the famous Paris banquet where he renounced his family titles he manifested a natural nobility of soul in his entire disinterestedness, professing no ambition but that of serving the public.

He superintended the efforts of the Irish agents to secure assitance from the French nation. His connection with the insurectionary movements was well known to the British authorities at an early date, but there was no haste made by local officials to issue the warrant for his arrest until everything was fixed for the outbreak. He succeeded in eluding the officers for two months after the other leaders were taken.

At length, on the 19th of May, he was captured after a desperate struggle, in which he received serious wounds. He died in prison on the 4th of June following.

"You said," broke in Tom, "that he took a part in the American war." "Is it possible that there were Irish soldiers fighting for England against the Americans?"

"Of their own free will and inclination I answer No!" replied the old man. "But, strange as it may appear, a body of 4,000 Irish troops formed part of the British force sent to put down the American colonists." "It happened as in many other foolish wars undertaken by England. The hapless Irishmen who had been entrapped into the ranks of the regular army were led to many a battle of which they did not approve.

The sentiments of the Irish people regarding this particular war were clearly made known to the world in the Irish Parliament when the King's demand for troops was under discussion.

On November 25th, 1774, this question was brought up. The few members in that body who honestly represented their country, were decidedly opposed to the project and expressed their views in the strongest language.

Ponsonby on this occasion declared: "If we give our consent we shall take part against America contrary to justice, to prudence, and to humanity."

Fitzgibbons, during the same debate, said: "The war is unjust, and Ireland has no reason to be a party therein."

Sir Edward Newenham could not agree to send more troops to butcher men who were fighting for their liberty."

George Ogle used the words: "If men must be sent to America, send there foreign mercenaries, not the brave sons of Ireland."

Hussey Bird condemned the American war as "a violation of the law of nations, the law of the land, the law of humanity, the law of nature; he would not vote a single sword without an address recommending conciliatory measures; the ministry, if victorious, would only establish a right to the harvest when they had burned the grain."

Yet the troops were voted by 121 against 76, although the resolution to replace them by foreign Protestants was negatived by 68 against 106. That Parliament was no longer a genuine Irish one. It was mainly a creature of the English ministers.

While the question was being agitated the merchants of Dublin publicly applauded the Earl of Effingham for "refusing to draw his sword against the lives and liberties of his fellow subjects in America."

In the same month, while the good wishes of the Irish people were thus manifested the first American Congress sent to Ireland a pledge of their unalterable sympathy and their joy that their own trials had extorted some mitigation of its wrongs.'

It was impossible to misunderstand the warm interest taken by the Irish people in the important question agitated among the promising nations across the Atlantic. A good proportion of the colonists were of Irish blood, while all were aware of the repeated efforts made in the old land to correct the same kind of abuses which they were now resisting.

Franklin, who had been the soul of the movement for colonial independence, submitted to Congress July 1st, 1775, an outline for confederating the colonies in one nation. In his scheme every colony of Great Britain in North America, and even Ireland, which was still classed with the colonies, was invited to accede to the union.

The next among our patriots deserving special notice here is Theobald Wolfe Tone.

He was born in Dublin June 20th, 1763. His education was completed at Trinity College, in his native city. After graduating from that eminent seat of learning he was called to the bar in London in the year 1787.

He soon became prominent as an advocate of liberal political measures. With a view to promoting reforms urgently needed in his native country he endeavored to unite the Catholics of Ireland with the Dissenters of England as a means of success in removing their grievances.

His ideas were presented to the public in a letter entitled, "An argument on behalf of the Catholics of Ireland." It was published in 1791. In this year also he took part in founding the society of "United Irishmen" in Belfast. In 1792 he was reported to the government as holding treasonable negotiations with the French.

Fearing arrest he fled to the United States in 1795, and sailed from that country for France in January, '96. By his exertions a

French fleet was equipped to aid in the Irish insurrection. This he accompanied, holding the rank of adjutant-general to Hoché, who was its commander. The invasion undertaken in December of the same year ended in failure on account of severe storms encountered at the entrance to Bantry Bay. Returning to France, he continued in military service for the two years following. In September, '98, a second squadron was organized through him for the assistance of his countrymen. Holding his former position in this armament he was intercepted on the coast of Donegal by an English fleet. In the encounter that followed he was defeated. Here he was taken prisoner and brought to Dublin, where, after a trial by courtmartial, he was sentenced to be hanged on November 12. While in prison he was overwhelmed by excessive despondency and caused his own death the day preceding that set for his execution.

His life, written by himself, including his political writings, was published subsequently by his son, William Theobald. The latter became a distinguished soldier in the French army. After the fall of Napoleon he went to the United States and continued the military profession under the flag of his adopted country.

One of the most distinguished of the leaders was Thomas Addis Emmet. He was born in Cork April 24th, 1764. Having graduated at Trinity College, Dublin, he pursued a course of medicine at the University of Edinburgh. Having visited the celebrated schools of the continent and selected the legal profession, a two years course was added at the Temple in London. He was admitted to the bar in 1791. His earnest devotion to all liberal projects in behalf of his native country brought him into universal popularity. In '96 he became associated with the organizers of the rebellion. Along with Arthur O'Connor, Dr. McNevin, a Dublin physician ,and Lord Edward Fitzgerald, he acted as executive director of the "United Irishmen."

On the information conveyed to government by a traitor named Thomas Reynolds, he was arrested on the 12th of March, '98, at his own house in Dublin. In July following, while in prison with other leaders on the same charge, it was agreed, at the suggestion of Samuel Neilson, to reveal the general secrets of their system, without inculpating individuals, on condition of gaining their liberty. Permisson to exile themselves to any country not at war with England was hereby granted.

The patriotic prisoners when giving the desired evidence before the committee of parliament, took occasion to justify the revolt of the country by their earnest denunciation of the glaring abuses sanctioned by the ministers. Instead of immediate liberation their term of imprisonment was prolonged for three more years. This latter period was spent by Emmet at Fort George in the Highlands of Scotland.

Under the kind hearted Colonel Stuart, who was then governor of the prison, our noble convict was allowed some unusual privileges. The gallant Scotch general relaxed the severity of ordinary prison life and treated him with the consideration due to his rank and accomplishments.

In 1802, after the treaty of Amiens, he was liberated on condition that he should settle in a foreign country and never attempt to return to his own. In company with his wife, who was granted the same permission on the same terms, he withdrew to France.

In the city of Brussels, where he had occasion to pass on his journey, he met his brother, Robert, who was also an exile, and engaged in the patriotic projects for which he afterwards became famous.

In 1804 Thomas Addis proceeded to the United States, of which he became a devoted citizen. He entered here on the profession of law, and soon attained eminence duly acknowledged by all classes.

His ability and integrity were attested by his appointment to the office of Attorney General of the State of New York in 1812.

His death occurred on November 14th, 1827, at his home in New York City. In the cemetery of St. Paul's on Broadway, lie his ashes; and the handsome monument conspicuous to the multitudes passing daily on that thoroughfare tells of the universal esteem he enjoyed among his fellow citizens. His descendants are numerous and inherit his abilities, while holding the highest rank in the social life of the great city where talent and worth never fail to be recognized.

While the virtues of the parent are continued in the children, that of patriotism is not wanting. Worthy sons of the honored exile are ready to promote by voice, and pen, and treasure the prosperity of the old land.

The best interests of a country for which so much blood was shed will not want for friends while the kindred of martyred patriots find a favorable moment for tendering their services.

The name of Robert Emmet, brother of the foregoing, should not be passed over while reviewing the prominent leaders of this period in Ireland. Although the agitation of which he was promoter, took place four years later than that of '98, yet he took an active part in both risings.

He was born in Dublin in the year 1780. Trinity College was the scene of his devotion to study, of his remarkable talents, and literary honors won among a group of fellow students all notably brilliant.

His ardent patriotism was manifested without reserve, and as an advocate of republican principles he came under censure of the college authorities. In the course of the political troubles of '98 he was dismissed from the institution with nineteen others suspected of similar liberal views.

When other leaders of the insurrection were arrested he was obliged to fly from the country, as he was equally implicated in their treasonable projects.

He escaped to France, where he remained until the armed revolt was quieted at home. But he was not there to be idle. Several other refugees joined him with untiring persistency in appeals to Napoleon for a sufficient invading force to aid their countrymen. This proud general, who was then First Consul of France and in absolute control of the military, entered seriously into negotiation with the exiles and kept them in hope. He intimated that a new war was soon to be declared against England. This would be their opportunity. They were encouraged to form a legion composed of all the exiles then in the country under command of Tone's trusty aide-de-camp, McSheehey, while Thomas Addis Emmet and Arthur O'Connor were to remain at Paris as plenipotentiaries of their nation. He even went so far as to suggest the colors and the motto under which they were to fight when once landed on their native soil. The flag, on a tricolor ground, was to have a green centre bearing the letters: R. I.—Republique Irlandaise. Their legend was to be "L'independence de l'Irlande"—"Liberte de Conscience."

It was his suggestion also to form an Irish committee at Paris, and to prepare statements of Irish grievances for the "Moniteur," and the semi-official papers.

Assured of Napoleon's good will for the Irish cause, and cheered by his repeated promises of aid, Robert Emmet secretly returned to Dublin in October, 1802, determined to reestablish in some degree the old organization of the United Irishmen.

In May, 1803, hardly a year after the proclamation of the peace of Amiens, the new war was declared between England and France.

Emmet now went about his work with energy and enthusiasm. Many kindred spirits shared in his views and seconded his efforts. Trusty emissaries were despatched to the different counties to wake up new ambition among the disheartened peasantry. His chief confidants were Thomas Russell and Mathew Dowdall, formerly prisoners at Fort George, but now permitted to return. James Hope of Templepatrick, was a ready co-worker, and Michael Dwyer, the former leader of Wicklow rebels, still surviving, uncaptured since '98, gave valuable assistance. Mr. Long, a Dublin merchant, furnished the sum of £1,400 to be used in purchasing war supplies. To this amount of treasure, Robert himself added £1,500 of his own private income. Depots of powder and arms were established in various parts of the city of Dublin and in the provinces north and west.

Favorable reports were received from many parts of the country. At least nineteen counties were prepared to rise as soon as the signal was given from Dublin. Robert's immediate scheme was to seize the Castle and arsenals and take possession of the city.

On the 23d of July he had mustered together a considerable body of insurgents hastily drilled and supplied with arms.

Under his leadership they marched through several streets with much display and evident warlike intentions. Chief Justice Kilwarden, whom they met driving in his carriage, was attacked and cruelly murdered. This was the only bloodshed permitted on that day. The regular troops from the various garrisons were promptly on the scene and dispersed the armed multitude.

Robert succeeded in escaping to the County Wicklow, where he remained concealed for some time, taking measures to notify other intending insurgents of his own failure and advising a postponement of their revolt for a more favorable season.

Of his associates in this enterprise fallen into the hands of the government officers Thomas Russell was executed at Downpatrick, while Kearney, Roche, Redmond and Howley were hanged in Dublin.

Many were imprisoned for different periods, and a few escaped to France.

Although facilities for leaving the country in safety were offered by friends, Robert could not be persuaded to depart without paying a visit to his lover, Miss Curran. Aware of the great risk in the journey he called back to the city for the desired farewell interview, was tracked and arrested.

After a public trial he was convicted of high treason and hanged on the 20th of September, 1803.

Of Robert Emmet's popularity among his countrymen and the admiration in which he was regarded for natural nobility of character we need only quote as proof the words of Thomas Moore, one of his college companions.

This friend said of him that of all his acquaintances no other possessed "in the greatest degree moral worth combined with intellectual power."

The famous speech which he delivered at his trial is admitted to be a model of pathetic eloquence never surpassed in any language.

At the many trials of political prisoners charged with treason for taking part in the insurrection there was one man who bore a conspicuous part and should be mentioned here. He was John Philpot Curran, the matchless orator and fearless advocate of patriots.

For his extraordinary gifts of oratory he deserves a place among the most eminent public men worthy of record in his country's history.

For his disinterested services in the defence of men for whom no clemency could be expected before the courts such as then existed in Ireland, his name is venerated by his countrymen as one of their greatest heroes.

He himself was not a rebel. He deplored the rashness of the young patriots and would have dissuaded them from an enterprise that he knew to be premature and hopeless. But

F

he knew their motives. He knew the humiliating and degraded condition of the people with the intolerable abuses under which they groaned and were driven to madness or despair. If he could not approve of their methods employed to right their wrongs, he was still aware that they had wrongs and abundant cause for attempting strong measures to save their country from a corrupt system of government.

In pleading their cause before a court that had all outward forms of an enlightened tribunal he hoped for no mitigation of the sentence expected from a jury whose mind was already made up.

Never was an advocate more intensely anxious to save his clients. His soul seemed to reflect in itself the sorrows of his prostrate people, and even with certainty of failure he may have sought consolation in giving vent to his anguish while vehemently denouncing a nation's wrongs before the impartial world for an audience.

The town of Newmarket, in the County Cork, was his birthplace.

From the date of his birth, July 24th, 1750, till the day of his death, October 14, 1817, there intervened an epoch of more melancholy aspect than any other of equal length in the political history of Ireland.

The whole machinery of government presented a horrid spectre of bribery and deceit. The ministry, the bench, the magistracy, represented the most shameless rapacity and bigotry. The feelings of humanity were blunted, conscience was blind, pity was deaf, but vengeance was all alive and all awake. Law was a dead letter, trial by jury was "a delusion, a mockery, and a snare."

Anyone who reads the records of those times will learn how universal was then in Ireland the reign of terror.

The Marquis of Cornwallis, Lord Lieutenant of Ireland, at the close of the insurrection, says that the executions of ordinary courts or courts martial, were nothing compared with the butcheries and burnings committed by armed and licensed murderers, who were as much detested by the humane among the rulers as they were monstrous and merciless to the people. In such a condition of things Curran had to stand almost alone. He had to speak for the speechless, when words for the accused were almost accounted crimes, and he had to take the side of the doomed when the rancour of party spirit often confounded the advocate with the client.

Curran, in 1794, while defending Dr. Drennan, who was prosecuted for a seditious libel, says in the course of his speech: "I have been parading through the capital, and I feel that the night of unenlightened wretchedness is fast approaching, when a man shall be judged before he is tried, when the advocate shall be libelled for discharging his duty to his client—that night of human nature, when a man shall be hunted down, not because he is a criminal, but because he is obnoxious."

In most of the state trials the law and the evidence were fearfully against Curran; and if they were not, packed and prejudiced juries were sure to be. This last circumstance seems to have caused him the severest labor and the sorest distress. The struggles of his genius when dealing with such juries suggest to us the struggle of a noble gladiator with beasts in the Roman circus. The gladiator knows that the beasts will kill him, but none the less he maintains his manhood to the last.

Curran, in the trials of 1798 encountered all sorts of dangers. He was hooted by the armed yeomanry, persecuted with anonymous letters, hated most heartily by officials and their slaves, by men made savage and cruel by their passions and their fears.

In the course of his profesional career he fought four duels. His first was with the Hon. Mr. St. Leger, brother to Lord Doneraile; the second with John Fitzgibbon, the Attorney-General for Ireland; the third, with Major Hobart, the Irish Secretary of State; the fourth, with a lawyer named Egan. The age he lived in was that of the pistol. Being also an age of political corruption he could not escape heated conflicts in the exercise of his profession. Being entirely fearless he persisted in the face of the most bitter hostility.

The power of his eloquence lay in his fervid appeals to the eternal laws of truth, of justice and of right implanted in human nature as long as that nature is not entirely depraved. His imagination, vivid and versatile, and his passion kindled by earnest conviction, aided his arguments to strike with telling force.

He used with adroitness the shafts of sarcasm and irony, and turned his antagonist into ridicule as the occasion demanded. He was fierce in his threats and denunciations and scornful reproaches against base motives, and again he could appeal to the tender emotions with a pathos that seldom failed to evoke tears even in an audience hostile to him.

When failing health made the duties of public office irksome he resigned the dignity of chancery judge, which he held from 1806, and sought repose in his quiet home at Brompton, near London. Here he died, having reached the age of sixty-seven years. No man ever carried to the grave a public reputation more free from blemish. His remains, after occupying a grave in London for 20 years, were transferred to Glasnevin Cemetery, near Dublin, where they now finally repose.

His countrymen in thus providing him with a tomb in their midst, gratify their deep affection for the man and fulfil the words he had uttered long before: "The last duties will be paid by that country on which they are devolved; nor will it be for charity that a little earth will be given to my bones. Tenderly will those duties be paid, as the debt of well-earned affection, and of gratitude not ashamed of her tears."

CHAPTER XI.

PROMINENT STATESMEN OF THE TIME.

A brief sketch of the men who held the highest government positions in Ireland during the period under consideration will have some interest.

Before noticing the ministers of the King in their disgraceful administration of Irish affairs we will first take a glance at the King himself.

George III., who reigned from 1760 to 1810, a period of fifty years, presents a fair sample of the arrogant ruler and politician of his time. There is nothing found of a successful feature in his whole reign except its great length. Political failures and humiliations were numerous, and to his obstinacy and extravagant royal pretentions the cause is attributed.

For a portion of his unlucky reign he had to be restrained as a lunatic and he ended his life in the same condition. His best friends would admit that his head was never well balanced. No wonder if his highest officials were guilty of blunders. There seemed to be in his day an epidemic of mismanagement as well as corruption among those in high places. In recording the character of the King we trace the follies of the officials who carried out his hated policy both at home and in the British colonies.

If the Irish people were asked to explain their grievances during the reign of George III, they might only repeat the complaint of the American colonists made to the world on July 4th, 1776. The language used by Jefferson in the immortal document, "The Declaration of Independence," ratified by the Congress of the United States, could be applied as if a congress of Irishmen were speaking.

Let us select a few of the many charges therein made against that detested monarch. In his first draft of that declaration Jefferson had written the following as charges against the King.

"He has waged war against human nature itself, violating its most sacred rights of life and liberty in the persons of a distant people who never offended him, captivating them and carrying them into slavery in another hemisphere, or to incur miserable death in their transportation thither.

"This piratical warfare, the opprobium of infidel powers, is the warfare of the Christian King of Great Britain." . . . He continues more of the charges thus: "The history of the present King of Great Britain is a history of repeated injuries and usurpations, all having in direct object, the establishment of absolute tyranny over those States. . . . . He has forbidden his governors to pass laws of immediate and pressing importance, unless suspended in their operation till his assent should be obtained, and when so suspended, he has utterly neglected to attend to them."

He has refused to pass other laws for the accommodation of large districts of people, unless those people would relinquish the right of representation in legislature—a right inestimable to them, and formidable to tyrants only. . . . . .

"He has endeavored to prevent the population of these States; for that purpose abstaining the laws of naturalization of foreigners, refusing to pass others to encourage their migration hither, and raising the conditions of new appropriations of lands."

"He has erected a multitude of new offices, and sent hither swarms of officers to harass our people and eat out their subsistence.

"He has kept among us in time of peace standing armies without the consent of our legislature.

"He has affected to render the military independent of, and superior to, the civil power. . . . . . . giving his assent to their (the Lords and Commons) acts of pretended legislature; for quartering large bodies of armed troops among us; for protecting them by mock trial from punishment for any murders which they should commit on the inhabitants of these States; for cutting off our trade with all parts of the world; for imposing taxes on us without our consent, etc.

"He is at this time transporting large armies of foreign mercenaries to complete the work of death, desolation, and tyranny, already begun, with circumstances of cruelty and perfidy, scarcely paralleled in the most barbarous ages, and totally unworthy the head of a civilized nation. .... He has excited domestic insurrections amongst us, and has endeavored to bring on the inhabitants of our frontiers, the merciless Indian savages, whose known rule of warfare is an undistinguished destruction of all ages, sexes, and conditions."

"In every stage of these oppressions we have petitioned for redress, in most humble terms; our repeated petitions have been answered only by repeated injuries. A prince whose character is thus marked by every act which may define a tyrant, is unfit to be ruler of a free people."

Many of the national disasters which humbled the pride of Britain in George's reign might have been averted if his arbitrary meddling in affairs of state could have been prevented.

The repeated demand of the Irish Catholics for their civil rights were neglected chiefly through his decided opposition. Indeed every attempt at reforming old abuses or introducing liberal measures in administration were thwarted at the hands of this self-willed and arbitrary tyrant.

His first symptoms of insanity betrayed themselves in 1758. In the spring of 1775 the patience of the Americans was exhausted, and they declared war with England.

The defeat and surrender of Burgoyne's army followed in '77. To add to the dishonor of England in this war the King's persistent policy of recruiting as many as possible of the American Indians to fight against the colonists was carried out. Mercenary troops from the German states of Hesse-Cassel and Brunswick were imported at great expense for the same purpose.

A new war with France began in the following year.

The final expulsion after capitulation of the English army under Cornwallis brought a fresh humiliation to Great Britain in 1782.

Then came the Irish revolt in '98, while in the same year England was engaged in another sanguinary war with the French army under Napoleon in the famous Egyptian campaign.

In 1809 a Jubilee celebration was observed in England in honor of the King's reign of 50 years. But in truth the British nation had not much cause for rejoicing, for almost the whole continent of Europe was just then under the rule of France. The King's malady returned in 1810. New disputes arose with the United States which threatened to add new disasters to the gloom and popular discontent prevailing at home.

When George ceased to be King at his relapse into insanity and was removed by death nine years later many others among his subjects were glad as well as the people of Ireland.

The English statesmen deputed by George III. as Lord Lieutenants of Ireland were seldom of a character to conciliate the disaffected inhabitants.

When any of them happened to show too much honesty in administration to suit the rapacious horde of minor officials and place-hunters he soon fell under their malignant censures, was reported to the royal advisers, as incompetent for the exigencies of his post of duty, and was consequently recalled.

An example of this rare quality of honest purpose in a Viceroy to Ireland we find in Lord Fitzwilliam.

His short administration of three months had won him the affections of the city of·Dublin, so that at his departure a popular demonstration was made of their feelings of respect and gratitude.

Thus the people proved that it was the arrogance and the rapacity of their rulers, and not the men themselves which embittered their minds and fostered disloyalty, whilst the slightest prospect of redress for their wrongs or gracious treatment secured their confidence.

As successor to Fitzwilliam Lord Camden was sent over in March, '95. He continued in the Viceregal office until June 21st, '98, and on account of the part he played in relation to the Irish rebellion his name may be allowed a place here.

Born in Devonshire in 1714, he was known by his family name as Charles Pratt. His education was obtained at Eton and Cambridge. As a profession he selected law and commenced its practice in 1738. His abilities recommended him for advancement in public life. His first appointment of distinction was as Attorney General, to which honor was added the title of Knight in 1757. On the accession of George III| in 1760 he was made Chief Justice of the Court of Common Pleas. In 1765 he was raised to the peerage under the name of Baron Camden.

The following year ('66) he was still further promoted by obtaining the post of Lord Chancellor. On May 13th, 1786, he was created Earl Camden. During the parliamentary debates on colonial matters he distinguished himself by advocating the rights of the Americans.

From the date of his arrival as Viceroy in '95 the Irish parliament relapsed into its old degenerate habits. In the House of Commons Grattan remained with a few of his liberal colleagues making a last effort at reforms.

The emancipation of the Catholics, repeatedly brought by him before the house, was rejected by a majority of ten to one. Instead of conciliatory measures there were several acts of coercion passed. Among them was the Insurrection Act, giving power to the magistrates of any county to proclaim martial law; the Riot Act, giving authority to disperse any number of persons by force of arms without notice; Suspension of the habeas corpus, &c.

The few patriotic members, now seeing their efforts useless and that parliament had become a mere tool in the hands of the oppressors of their country, decided to withdraw, formally and openly from further attendance on the House of Commons. Along with Grattan in this resolution were George Ponsonby, Curran, Hardy, Lord Edward Fitzgerald, Lord Henry Fitzgerald, Arthur O'Connor and others.

Grattan's solemn admonition on this occasion ended with these affecting words: "We have offered you our measure—you will reject it; we deprecate yours—you will persevere; having no hopes left to persuade or to dissuade, and having discharged our duty, we shall trouble you no more, and after this day shall not attend the House of Commons."

In a letter to Castlereagh in '93 Lord Camden betrayed the English policy of goading the Irish people into insurrection in order to deprive them of their liberties. He faithfully carried out the instructions that he received from the King, at his appointment, "to support the old English interest as well as the Protestant religion." He was responsible also for the "quartering of the soldiers among the peasantry and all the horrors following from such practices.

A brave and fair minded Scotch general, Sir Ralph Abercrombie, who was in command of the military forces, resigned his post in disgust at the atrocious conduct of the magistracy and military officers in dealing with the defenseless people. Camden accepted his resignation and allowed the abuses to continue with Lord Lake holding temporary command.

Lord Cornwallis was appointed Lord Lieutenant of Ireland to succeed Camden June 21st, '98. He was sent with the two-fold authority of civil and military service. His reputation as a British general was long established both in his own country and abroad. He was born December 31st, 1738. At the famous English seats of learning, Eton and Cambridge, he received his education.

He entered the army at an early age, and had ample opportunity to exercise his military abilities in the various campaigns which occupied England at that period. In the seven years' war he did great service under Lord Granby, and was honored with the peerage in 1762.

As a statesman he showed some liberal tendencies in opposing the measures which led to the American war.

Although disapproving the British policy of provoking the colonies to resistance he had to engage in the armed conflict when war was declared. With his regiment he accompanied the fleet that was despatched to reinforce the forces under Howe and Clinton in their campaigns against the American insurgents. He held the post of major-general while planning assaults on the enemy in New Jersey, and commanded the detachment that took possession of Philadelphia September 24th, 1777. The siege of Charleston in 1780 was conducted by him. After its capture he continued in command of about 4,000 troops to control the disaffected of South Carolina. He gained a victory over Gates at Camden August 16th, 1780, and a second over Greene at Guilford March 15th, 1781.

After this he met various reverses, and at Yorktown, being unable to escape by sea, he shut himself up behind strong intrenchments to repel the enemy. Here he was surorunded by the Americans, combined with the French fleet recently arrived as allies. After some show of resistance he was forced to surrender with his whole force October 19th, 1781.

This event put an end to the war. It led to the change in the English ministry and the recognition of American independence.

Having returned with his regiment to England he was despatched to new scenes of warfare in India, and in 1786 was appointed governor general and commander-in-chief of the English army in Bengal.

Recalled to England, his services were recognized by other marks of royal favor, and in '98 he was selected for the position of Viceroy in Ireland. The insurrection was at its height on his arrival. His instructions were similar to those given to Camden—to bring about the abolition of the Irish parliament while thoroughly subduing the insurgents. He assumed the task with zeal, using all the authority and resources at his command to completely disarm the people. With the powerful reinforcements of military then distributed in every section of the country, an experienced general as he was could not claim great merit for bringing the rebellion to a close.

It is but just to acknowledge that his administration was marked by efforts on his part to repress the excesses of the Orange party and lessen the brutal conduct of the military officials that had long distracted the inhabitants under his predecessors.

He continued as Lord Lieutenant of Ireland attending diligently to state affairs, and winning the favor of the royal master for two years after the rebellion was suppressed. He had the distinction of presiding at the successful scheme of union between Ireland and Great Britain in 1800. His resignation of the office was handed to the King in 1801. The next service to his country performed by him was the ratification of the peace of Amiens, for which he was deputed to France as plenipotentiary in 1802.

Lastly his military abilities marked him out for a second appointment as general in India. Arriving in Calcutta to resume that important part of duty in 1805, death put an end to his career.

Another notorious figure during the period of Irish revolt was Lord Castlereagh. In the beginning of '98 he became Chief Secretary of Ireland, and to him is due the most disreputable part of government intrigues both to provoke the country into rebellion and afterwards to abolish the Irish parliament. It is not in approval of any acts of his public life, as far as they related to Ireland, that a sketch of his career finds a place here. We merely put him on record as a curiosity of human degradation and depravity detested by his countrymen, whether co-temporaries with him or who have lived since to recall his memory.

His family name was Robert Stewart, and his civil titles borne during his political career was Marquis and Viscount of Londonderry.

He was born at the family seat of Mount Stewart, County Down, Ireland, June 18th, 1769. In his youth he attended the grammar school at Armagh and completed his education at Cambridge University.

Early in life he had ambition for political honors, and in 1789 he succeeded in being elected to the Irish parliament as a member for the County Down.

In the sharp contest at that election his family was said to have spent the large sum of £25,000; such was the method of securing votes among the aristocracy of that period. In 1794 he was returned to the British House of Commons, and again in '96 secured a seat as member for Oxford.

Relinquishing his honors in the English parliament, he secured re-election for the County Down in Ireland, and was appointed Keeper of the Privy Seal.

Appointed Chief Secretary to Lord Cornwallis in '98, he was chief adviser in the repressive policy of the Castle, and actively encouraged the abuses among the military magistrates.

After the Union was accomplished he retired to England, entering the first Imperial Parliament both for 1801 and 1802. Various positions of honor were conferred upon him from this time forward, such as Privy Councillor of Great Britain, and President of the Board of Control, Secretary of War for the Colonies, &c.

In 1809, after encountering much political opposition and taking part in heated debates on public affairs he fell under bitter censure on account of a foolish expedition to Walcheren that ended in disgraceful failure.

From 1812 to 1820 he held a seat in parliament for his native County Down. His support of George IV. in his efforts to get rid of Queen Caroline, and his repeated opposition to popular measures increased the general feelings of contempt with which he was regarded by all except the narrow circle around the throne. He fell into a state of melancholy at his country seat in Kent, England, and cut his throat with a penknife, thus finding a miserable death August 12th, 1822.

Charles James Fox was an English statesman and orator who had a notable influence in public affairs during the period in which he lived. He was born in London January 24th, 1749. On his mother's side he was a descendant of Charles II. and Henry IV. of France. From Eton, where his studies commenced, he went to Oxford in 1764, and there made a brilliant record for superior natural gifts. From the University he went to the continent to gratify his literary tastes, where he found ample opportunities. Returning to England, he entered a parliamentary career in which his influence was exercised for the introduction of liberal principles.

He foretold the defeat of the British arms in America after making a vigorous plea in behalf of the colonists.

In 1782 he was made Secretary for Foreign Affairs, and undertook to secure peace with the hostile powers and the recognition of the Independence of the United States. Parliamentary reform was earnestly advocated by him in conjunction with Pitt, who was minister at that time.

Concessions to Ireland he also insisted on with his usual eloquence. In 1788 he joined Burke and Windham in opening the impeachment of Warren Hastings for his Indian barbarities.

In 1797 he retired from the active debates of Parliament on account of the overwhelming majority opposed to every motion for reform.

In 1798 he was put off the list of Privy Councillors for having repeated the Duke of Norfolk toast: "To the majesty of the people."

By his efforts in the House of Commons he secured a vote for the abolition of the slave trade, and negotiated the peace with France.

With generous purpose he labored with Wilberforce and Burke to further every project in the cause of humanity.

To his influence are due the various measures of reform in the constitution, which have finally been adopted.

Ireland's grievances as well as those of the American colonists, were painted in their true colors in his fervid appeals to his countrymen.

Mackintosh says of him: "He certainly possessed above all moderns that union of reason, simplicity, and vehemence which formed the prince of orators. He was the most Demosthenian speaker since Demosthenes."

To review the career of such a man is a work most gratifying to the historian, who too often has the repulsive task of tracing characters of an ignoble type.

In Fox's day corruption among politicians and men in places of public trust was the general rule, and it required a courage more than ordinary to stand forth as the champion of popular rights or any liberal measures. Fox had a soul far above all petty considerations of self-interest. His character may be summed up as follows: He was thoroughly disinterested, and sought only the honor of his country and the greatest good of humanity. He died at Chiswick September 13th, 1806.

CHAPTER XII.

THE UNION OF IRELAND WITH GREAT BRITAIN.

To rob Ireland of her parliament was the purpose of George III. and his ministers in provoking the Irish people into armed rebellion. That object was accomplished in the second year after the revolt was suppressed.

Of course it was said that the Irish gave up their parliament willingly by a regular vote of their representatives in the House of Commons at their own capital. To say so would be far from the truth. The measure was resisted by all true Irishmen with the greatest determination. What was made to appear a voluntary surrender was nothing but a base sham.

When a robber seizes your goods his act is no less a robbery because by administering noxious drugs he induces you, in your helpless condition, to say you bestow them.

The infamous methods employed by the King's ministers to influence a few so-called Irish legislators assembled in Dublin are no less detestable than the operations of the burglar to secure his neighbor's treasure.

What is called "packing a jury" is admitted by everyone to be a most disgraceful way of accomplishing a purpose. It means that the most effective way of obtaining justice is perverted into an instrument of inflicting wrong. The jurymen are selected on account of their one-sided sympathy either well known from former habit or purchased at a price. No one will take their decision as worthy of respect, notwithstanding that their case is conducted under the forms of law.

For similar reasons the acts of the Irish Parliament, at the period under consideration, do not deserve to be called independent legislation, and are grossly disreputable.

Lord Cornwallis, after crushing the rebellion by his military activity, began at once to exercise his abilities and powers as legislator.

Faithful to his master, the King, as a successful general he wanted to show his devotion to the royalist interests in his acts as Lord Lieutenant.

He set his mind to the task of making Ireland a mere province of the British empire by abolishing its independent parliament. The great plea used by him and other advocates of the measure was, "the consolidation of the British Empire."

On the 22d of June, 1799, he presented his plans before the assembled parliament. He congratulated both houses on the suppression of the late rebellion, on the defeat of Bompart's squadron, and the recent French victories of Nelson, and proceeded to unfold his project for the union of their body with that of England.

On the paragraph in his address referring to the Union, a debate commenced in the Commons which lasted till one o'clock the following day—more than twenty consecutive hours.

Against the Union spoke Ponsonby, Parsons, Fitzgerald, Barrington, Plunkett, Lee, O'Donnell and Bushe.

In its favor the advocates were Lord Castlereagh, Corry, Fox, Osborne, Duignan and some others.

The contest was carried on in the English Parliament as well as in Dublin. The two great parties engaged in the discussion were known as "Unionists" and "Anti-Unionists."

That there was a "Unionist" party in Ireland may cause surprise to those who are unacquainted with the state of the country at that period.

All wonder will vanish when it is recollected that the whole island was overrun with a greedy multitude of officials of various kinds in the pay of the government; a host of Church of England clergymen; a rapacious body of the legal profession, as well as the landlord class with their numerous agents—nearly all of English importation.

As these were all in quest of the fat things only that they derived from the nation their minds were little concerned about the country's political independence or its commercial prosperity. As long as their various revenues were assured they lent their aid in promoting English interests, completely deaf to the appeals of the natives for a remedy of their grievances. The landlord class alone wielded a power that was felt in every corner of the island. They were for the most part absentees, i.e., they lived out of the country, generally in their sumptuous castles of England or Scotland, or seeking amusement while squandering their wealth in the European capitals.

To them Ireland was a place not worth thinking of except as far as its estates yielded them a revenue. Their faithful agents who had the collecting of their revenues, lived in luxury hardly less than that of their masters, and were a formidable colony for English interests at Ireland's capital.

The tenantry on the estates owned by the absentee landlord were completely at the mercy of the agent. At his bidding the tenant cast his vote. If he dare assert his right of choice his fate was well known. It meant the loss of his home—eviction from the land to which he is attached by all the ties of affection—a home sacred by the memories of a venerable ancestry.

The merits of the candidate for parliament were not to be considered in the case. The candidate might be a county squire of well known depraved habits, as often was the case, and without capacity for any public office. If he was the choice of the landlord the matter was decided by instructions issued by the agent on election day.

Another powerful instrument of the English

government in Ireland was the Established Church. This embraced the body of bishops and inferior clergy with the richly endowed colleges.

As the bishops were selected by the King, and held the rank of Lords in the Irish Parliament, they always turned the scale in the Upper House in favor of every act dictated from the throne. They, along with the numerous ministers in charge of so-called parishes throughout the country, represented extensive land ownership, while Trinity College enjoyed enormous revenues from wide estates confiscated from the old Catholic proprietors.

Catholics were allowed to dwell on the land once owned by their ancestors on condition of paying rents to those new masters in order that the State Church might flourish. But their presence as tenants was not desired and was only tolerated as a source of profit. Whenever enough of Scotch settlers or other adventurers were found to take the land on the same terms the native residents were forced to fly into exile.

That a clergy so liberally provided for by the government should be loyal is not difficult to understand. The salaries of the Church of England bishops—the creatures of the King, were so large that the office of bishop was one of the most desirable in the Kingdom.

The salary of the ordinary Protestant parson was enough to secure him the enjoyment of luxuries more than ordinary, while elegant residences with choice acres of glebe-lands were also provided for them by the same bountiful state treasury.

The ranks of the clergy, it need not be added, were well filled. Many an English nobleman having more sons than he could provide for at home, found it very convenient to place one or two of his genteel boys in one of those Irish church livings. Indeed, the life of these sleek parsons could not be called Apostolic. For, the bishop lived in a sumptuous style in some lovely palace, with title of an imaginary diocese in some corner of Catholic Munster or Connaught, without any Protestant flock, while the inferior country parsons found life equal to a perpetual vacation.

Other officials enjoying comfortable government positions were tax collectors, spies, contractors and traders for supplying the numerous military garrisons. English merchants also swarmed in the chief seaports.

If we add to this foreign element the influence of judges, lawyers, and various petty officers of the court, there will appear material enough to form a party whose tastes and feelings incline to the so-called "consolidation of the British empire."

The people of Dublin, who always embodied the sentiments of the whole country, showed how anxious they were about the fate of their native parliament. Bad as it proved itself to be for years past and almost beyond hope of reform, it was, nevertheless, to their minds a symbol, if nothing more, of their independence as a nation. Its abolition foreboded evils still more disastrous.

During the debate on January 22d, mentioned above the galleries and lobbies of the House were crowded all night by the most prominent people of the city, including many ladies, with attention strained to the utmost to await the result of the vote.

That part of the Viceroy's address referring to the Union, was rejected by only one vote. There was public rejoicing at this announcement. The leading anti-Unionists were escorted in triumph to their homes, while the Unionists were protected by strong military escorts from the popular indignation. At night the city was illuminated, and the event was celebrated as a great victory.

Among the various arguments against the Union eloquently presented by the patriotic members was the convincing one of the incompetency of parliament to put an end to its own existence.

On this point Plunkett, in the course of his speech, exclaimed: "Yourselves you may extinguish, but parliament you cannot extinguish. It is enthroned in the hearts of the people—it is enshrined in the sanctuary of the constitution—it is immortal as the island that protects it. As well might the frantic suicide imagine that the act which destroys his miserable body should also extinguish his eternal soul. Again, therefore, I warn you, do not dare to lay your hands on the constitution—it is above your powers."

The defeated Unionists saw that it would be necessary to defer the matter for a time. But measures were taken for the final success of the project. The majority in the House which thwarted the Union must be got rid of, and for this purpose various schemes were set in motion. New members must be secured to the number of forty or fifty, who would be at the bidding of the Chief Secretary. New peerages were created, and other lucrative offices distributed among those whose votes were to be used as the Castle dictated. Vast sums of "secret service money" were employed in removing opposition. Those whose private interests were threatened by a change from a national to an imperial parliament were quieted by an advance of money large enough to compensate for all losses incurred through the new political changes. Great borough proprietors, like Lord Ely and Lord Shannon, received as much as £45,000 sterling in "compensation" for their loss of patronage, while proprietors of single seats received £15,000.

It is well known that the majority in both houses was purchased, while some were purchased twice over.

Lord Carysfort, an active partisan of the measure, writing in February, 1800, to his friend, the Marquis of Buckingham, frankly says: "The majority, which has been bought at an enormous price, must be bought over again before all the details can be gone through."

Inside of six months in that year there appeared in the Dublin "Gazette" a list of forty-two new peerages created by the arbitrary act of government in order to secure the needed majority in support of the Union.

That mysterious agency called "secret service fund" employed in the machinery of most governments, suggests some questions that might well make us blush for human nature. If all the dark deeds perpetrated under the pretense of national emergency through the "secret service fund" were exposed to public gaze what a ghastly picture of corruption in high places—of vile motives in so-called statesmen would be revealed!

The use of such money in Ireland was not only in purchasing the votes of the native citizens or legislators that they might betray their country's interests. The employment of spies at a high price was a long-continued system. Men of depraved tendencies found a profitable calling in the betrayal of most respectable citizens during the long years when the penal laws were in force. The trade of the "priest hunter" and the detective for reporting Catholics found engaged in their highest form of worship became profitable and gave occupation to a vile herd among the lowest dregs of the population. During the long reigns of Elizabeth and James and Charles that class of degraded humanity flourished. For a high price was placed on a priest's head, and every Catholic found at his devotions had to pay a high forfeit.

Another tool of the Castle government was the emissary paid to foster disunion, to stir up quarrels among the populace, to organize riots and disorders in order to furnish a pretense for severe legislation, and an excuse for delaying the country's demands for civil rights.

The money spent in this manner was charged to the Irish tax payer, so that he was forced to pay the vile wretch who helped to take away the liberties of his country. The treasury of the nation was made to do duty to keep the nation in bondage. Popular or treasonable agitation was fostered in order to excuse the repressive measures repeatedly decreed against the agitators. A spirit of jealousy and strife between the native princes was kept alive so that division would continue among the people, and thus their power for resisting oppression rendered feeble.

This stirring up of strife among the simple peasantry, this fomenting disunion and encouraging disorder for purposes of state policy was a business carried on with greater secrecy, and the lavish use of the "secret service fund" was generally kept carefully from public notice. But these dark proceedings are no longer secrets.

Subsequent history has revealed all these machinations of the politicians of former times so revolting to honest men and so disgraceful to any civilized government.

Where a noxious viper is nourished for the sake of the deadly mischief it is employed to inflict, the venom so carefully propogated will, in time, turn its bitterness against its employer and create an ulcer in the hand that brought it into life.

Dishonorable schemes in the ruler are soon copied by the common citizen, and the injured multitude will not fail to employ similar tactics in seeking a restoration of their rights.

Instead of elevating the subject, as the aim of civilized government should be; instead of legislating to promote civic and domestic virtues in the community, we find in the Irish administration an infernal machinery set at work to foster lying and deceit, to foment bitter animosities, and hinder the nation's prosperity.

When the Irish Parliament met again on the 15th of January, 1800, the plans of Castlereagh for securing a decisive vote for the Union appeared complete. The usual formalities were carried out. The Viceroy absenting himself, Lord Castlereagh read the message, and briefly sketched the plan of the Union. He congratulated the country on the improvement which had taken place in public opinion since the former session. He repeated the many advantages that would certainly follow from a United British Parliament in which Irish interests could be duly considered. He tried to dispel the fears of the different sections of the opposition party. The church establishment was to be secured, a vague promise was hinted that the Catholics would be emancipated, the commercial prosperity was sure to advance, while many beautiful changes for the better were enumerated.

Now began the debate with all the vigor witnessed within the same walls the preceding year. Through the long hours of the winter's night an eloquent war was maintained.

The scene is described by Sir Jonah Barrington, who was himself a distinguished actor in the struggle. "Every mind," says he, "was at its stretch, every talent was in its vigor; it was a momentous trial, and never was so general and so deep a sensation felt in any country.

Numerous British noblemen and commoners were present at that and the succeding debate, and they expressed opinions of Irish eloquence which they had never before conceived, nor ever after had an opportunity of appreciating. Every man on that night seemed to be inspired by the subject. Speeches more replete with talent and energy, on both sides, never were heard in the Irish Senate; it was a vital subject.

The sublime, the eloquent, the figurative orator, the plain, the connected, the metaphysical reasoner, the classical, the learned, and solemn declaimer, in a succession of speeches so full of energy and enthusiasm, so interesting in their nature, so important in their consequence, created a variety of sensations even in the bosom of a stranger, and could scarcely fail of exciting some sympathy with a nation which was doomed to close for ever that school of eloquence which had so long given character and celebrity to Irish talent."

After the discussion lasted eighteen hours a division was taken.

A majority of 42 was for the Union.

The new measure continued to be debated in committee up to the 21st of May, when Castlereagh got his bill accepted in the Irish House of Commons by a majority of sixty, and on the 7th of June it was finally passed.

The closing scene on this solemn occasion is described by Barrington as follows: "The galleries were full, but the change was lamentable. They were no longer crowded with those who had been accustomed to witness the eloquence and to animate the debates of that devoted assembly. A monotonous and melancholy murmur ran through the benches; scarcely a word was exchanged amongst the members; nobody seemed at ease; no cheerfulness was apparent; and the ordinary business, for a short time, proceeded in the usual manner.

"At length the expected moment arrived; the order of the day for the third reading of the bill for a 'legislative union between Great Britain and Ireland' was moved by Lord Castlereagh. Unvaried, tame, cold-blooded, the words seemed frozen as they issued from his lips; and, as if a simple citizen of the world, he seemed to have no sensation on the subject.

"At that moment he had no country, no

God, but his ambition. He made his motion, and resumed his seat, with the utmost composure and indifference.

"Confused murmurs again ran through the house. It was visibly affected. Every character, in a moment seemed involuntarily rushing to its index—some pale, some flushed, some agitated—there were few countenances to which the heart did not despatch some messenger. Several members withdrew before the question could be repeated, and an awful, momentary silence succeeded their departure. The speaker rose slowly from that chair which had been the proud source of his honors and of his high character. For a moment he resumed his seat, but the strength of his mind sustained him in his duty, though his struggle was apparent. With that dignity which never failed to signalize his official actions, he held up the bill for a moment in silence. He looked steadily around him on the last agony of the expiring parliament. He at length repeated, in an emphatic tone, 'as many as are of opinion that this bill do pass, say ay.' The affirmative was languid, but indisputable. Another momentary pause ensued. Again his lips seemed to decline their office.

"At length, with an eye averted from the object he hated, he proclaimed, with a subdued voice, 'The ayes have it.' The fatal sentence was now pronounced. For an instant he stood statue-like; then indignantly, and with disgust, flung the bill upon the table, and sank into his chair with an exhausted spirit. An independdent country was thus degraded into a province. Ireland as a nation was extinguished."

The number of Irish representatives allowed to take part in the Imperial Parliament in London was fixed at one hundred, and of peers to be elected for life was thirty.

The Church of England was declared as one with the Irish branch, and to be sustained on a similar footing with undiminished revenues.

The debt of Ireland in 1797 was less than £4,000,000. In '99 it was increased to £14,000,000, and it rose to £17,000,000 in 1801—all chargeable to Ireland alone.

On the 1st of January, 1801, a new imperial standard was displayed on London Tower, Edinburgh Castle and Dublin Castle. It took the form of the three combined crosses of St. Patrick, St. Andrew and St. George, under the popular title of the "Union Jack."

The purposes of the insurrection were now accomplished to the satisfaction of the King and his advisers.

In justice to all parties it must be recorded that among English statesmen there were some who opposed the Union and the reprehensible means employed to effect it. When speaking with an Irish acquaintance on the subject some time previously, Samuel Johnson declared his honest conviction, saying: "Do not unite with us, sir, it would be the union of the shark with his prey; we should unite with you to destroy you."

The gruff old Englishman was right. There were no advantages for Ireland derived from the Union.

If the promises made by the ministry had been promptly carried out—if the old abuses had been eradicated, and the country's prosperity given consideration, there is no doubt but the people of Ireland would have become reconciled to the new mode of legislation forced upon them. But nothing was done to conciliate the country without bitter and protracted agitation.

The emancipation of the Catholics was opposed by the King, and they were doomed to groan under the old load of disabilities for twenty-nine long years further until, by O'Connell's agitation, the concessions demanded were made at last.

The various acts of coercion that were passed in the British Parliament even after the Union—the increase in the military forces, and the strengthening of the garrisons over the country may be partly explained by the fears yet remaining lest France would resume her alliance with the Irish and attempt her former designs on the Kingdom.

Napoleon was reported to be deliberating with the exiled rebels, who had been welcomed by him and secured responsible positions in his powerful army.

The sympathy of the French nation for Ireland was well proved, while hostilities against England were only interrupted in order to await a new opportunity.

No wonder that suspicion lurked in the British camp. The thief holds his plunder with an uneasy conscience.

The regular paid and armed militia in the country now numbered 50,000 men, while 70,000 volunteers were enrolled, and battalioned and ready to be called out in case of emergency. To this formidable force an additional army of sea-fencibles were added.

It soon became plain that all the fine promises made would be disregarded, and that, great as the difficulties were before to get a hearing for Irish claims, still greater obstacles would be placed in the way of securing favorable legislation.

The struggle of Ireland to secure control of its own legislation may be compared to that of the American colonies during the early part of their history. The similarity appears especially striking in the new communities of Massachusetts and Virginia.

The arguments used by them were quite clear, and are equally forcible to-day. The English monarch and parliament claimed the right to appoint a governor or a commission to control the colonists without consulting their wishes.

The candidate selected for the office was generally sent directly from England, and was usually ignorant of the conditions of the newly settled country. He was seldom expected to have sympathy for the aspirations of the people, and assumed his new duties with the prospect of acquiring wealth at the expense of the struggling colonists, whom he was deputed to rule. The right to appoint these governors without the consent of the colonists was always vigorously disputed by them. Remonstrances were repeatedly sent over to England against such encroachments on their rights. Deputies were often chosen at their counsels to make the difficult journey and plead their case before parliament and beg to be relieved of the old grievance.

It is interesting to quote their own words when declaring their views on this matter in one of their pleas despatched to the English King. It is in the quaint manner of expression as used by one of the New England colonies, and is as follows: "There is more likelihood that such as are acquainted with the clime and its accidents may upon better grounds prescribe our advantages than such as shall sit at the helm in England."

This plea suits the case of Ireland exactly, and substantially embodies all her reasons for asking to be allowed to govern herself.

The colony of Virginia had for a long time resisted the royal pretensions. The struggle was continued with great bitterness for many years. Even armed rebellion was the outcome of long continued oppression, and the impoverished settlers never willingly submitted to the authority either of the deputy or the commissioners sent from England to rule them.

But the mother country sustained its governor in the exercise and the emoluments of his office even at the cost of much bloodshed and devastation.

We cannot help observing that the old, favorite method of tyrants was employed there also to keep down the aspirations of the people for progressive institutions.

To restrict the education of the people, to keep them in ignorance was the state policy of the mother country, as we know from official documents of that period.

Even the few clergymen in the colony were considered dangerous because they ventured to express freely their opinions of the greedy adventurers who came over under royal supervision.

In 1761 William Berkeley, one of the most arrogant of these governors, set over Virginia by royal patent, wrote to a fellow adventurer of his own class: "The ministers should pray oftener and preach less. But, I thank God, there are no free schools, nor printing, and I hope we shall not have, these hundred years; for learning has brought disobedience, and heresy, and libels against the best government. God keep us from both."

In 1683 Charles II. instructed Virginia's governor not to allow any printing press in the colony on any pretense whatever.

The same rule was enforced under James II.

Massachusetts had a similar experience. In 1686, when Joseph Dudley was sent there as governor he was instructed to tolerate no printing press, while sustaining authority by force.

The old British idea of rule for Ireland was the same. Much would be gained, it was thought, if the great multitude was kept in ignorance. To hide from them the extent of their degradation would facilitate the arbitrary administration of government such as prevailed at the time.

From the first introduction of British dominion in Ireland under Henry VIII., when that profligate monarch pillaged the numerous religious houses of education, there was no pretense of providing schools for the common people until some years after the Union. Not until the year 1840 was that feeble attempt made at providing general education such as was styled the national system, which up to the present day has proved itself illiberal and inadequate to the wants of the people.

CHAPTER XIII.

CAUSES OF DISSENSION AMONG IRISH PATRIOTS.

A question naturally arises here which deserves a place in the records of Ireland's persistent efforts to secure her liberty.

To what causes can we trace so many failures in her resistance to oppression? Or, rather, why those frequent exhibitions of dissension in the nation's councils and action? What explains the latter will explain all.

It may be said by some that those dissensions may be traced to an innate fickleness, or irritability, or quarrelsome tendency peculiar to the Irish natural temperament—called by hostile critics an inborn perversity.

Even those who justly admire the well known virtues and genial disposition of the Irish race often find apparent grounds for taking this unfavorable view of the case. However, in order to be fair in forming a judgment on the matter the condition of the country with the various conflicting interests of its population should be thoroughly known. This applies especially to the most noted periods of public agitation. When the circumstances are duly weighed it will be evident that whatever appears fickle or turbulent in the national character is due to causes from outside, and was the result of long continued humiliations and grievous wrongs inflicted by an alien, dominant race.

There were two principal causes or fruitful sources of dissension, and both were forced on the country by the foreign government with deliberate and selfish purpose.

One of these elements of discord consisted in the introduction of a considerable foreign population during the periods of confiscation under James I. and Oliver Cromwell, as well as others of an earlier date.

The other fertile source of disunion was found in the introduction of a new religion which the native Irish refused to accept, and the aggravating methods employed by the English government to force that religion on the nation. We will consider both of these separately.

By the confiscation of the Irish land and the transferring of it to foreign adventurers the first foundation was laid for disunion among the inhabitants.

Those new owners of the soil proved to be a greedy horde of unscrupulous strangers without sympathy for the rights of the natives. They came by right of conquest and by royal authority. They came as intruders, and in the eyes of the original proprietors were regarded as little less than robbers. There were two distinct classes of newcomers. One class comprised the landlords, who as favorites of royalty got possession of those valuable estates with absolute control of their revenues. The other class was made up of tenants who volunteered to engage in agriculture with the obligation of paying a fixed annual rent to the new proprietor.

Neither of these classes of adventurers could be expected to have any sympathy with the rightful owners, whom they came to supplant in the enjoyment of estates endeared to the natives by ties of the dearest associations and the memories of a long ancestry.

This foreign element in the population reached considerable proportions in the northern province of Ulster. Here the plantations under James I were firmly established in the most fertile sections. In other parts of the island new additions to the foreign colonies were settled after the invasion and victories of Cromwell.

After the frightful butcheries of this fanatical conqueror whole districts became depopulated. He assumed the role of a second Joshua specially commissioned by the Lord to eradicate what he called the idolatrous inhabitants. Believing himself the instrument of Divine wrath on a doomed people, he entered upon the work of extermination without pretending to spare either sex or age more than the Jewish warriors spared the Philistines.

He proved himself an adept in discovering among the pages of Bible history certain passages that seemed to justify the cruelties of war. But such horrors as he perpetrated on the Irish people could not be found recorded among the achievements of any conqueror before his time, and must have originated in the depths of his own hypocritical and bloodthirsty soul.

What fire and sword did not accomplish in the wholesale carnage wherever he set his foot the horrors of banishment completed, so that the hated race might be got rid of. By his order whole shiploads of the hapless native Catholics were hastily dispatched to the Barbadoes and other islands of the West Indian group.

During the five years of this dictator's arbitrary rule even the English people themselves were filled with alarm for their liberties. They looked on dumbfounded at his audacity and military success, reluctantly submitting for the time to the humiliations brought on them by the fanatical ambition of one man, persuaded that the season of delirium would blow over and the nation be restored to rational order.

By the devastations wrought in Ireland by Cromwell's troops new territory was opened up for fresh adventurers from England. The vacant estates were offered by the conqueror as valuable prizes to his countrymen who had proved their loyalty either by favoring his policy at home or by faithful military service in his recent campaigns.

He even sent across the Atlantic a message to the Puritan colonists who had settled in Massachusetts kindly inviting them to return and occupy the beautiful valleys in Ireland which he had lately subdued. Those hardy pioneers on the American coast were reported as suffering much hardship in establishing new homes on a barren soil and amidst unreclaimed forests. But they were not ready to admit their enterprise to be a failure, and thankfully declined the sympathetic offers of Cromwell.

Others were found among his English friends at home numerous enough to accept the rich lands so lavishly bestowed by the dictator.

Of course it was from the ranks of the Puritans he selected those favorites as long as they could be found. They were like himself, fanatics in their religious views, if not equally unblushing hypocrites. Their qualities did not make them an improvement on the earlier brood of settlers, or more desirable neighbors for the Catholic peasantry.

Among them there was no pretence to conciliate the old race, whom they regarded as the victims of divine wrath, and now helplessly reduced to subjection as a despised remnant of an idolatrous nation.

To drive all the natives from the country, even were it possible, did not appear good policy, for the new proprietors saw no advantage in leaving their estates uncultivated where the supply of foreign tenants became insufficient. For their own interests, therefore, the landlords allowed the dispossessed natives to remain as tenants and enjoy the doubtful consolation of tilling the soil, even with the burden of dividing the products of their labor with strange masters.

With infinite patience the humble peasantry resigned themselves to their hard lot. Generation after generation they paid tribute to their foreign and hostile landlords. As peaceful, law-abiding husbandmen, they drew from the soil the heavy rents so sternly exacted; and when crops failed without their fault, and eviction followed with all its horrors, they said "good bye" to the old homestead of their fathers with a grief which only those of their own race can understand. The only choice for them was exile. They betook themselves to the emigrant ship to seek a welcome where lordly oppression had lost its power forever, and where they could enjoy the fruits of their industry secure from the hands of a rapacious and idle aristocracy.

Well meaning observers might say: "Far better would it have been for the Irish people if the entire race had fled from those cruel oppressions, and cast their lot on the new continent across the Atlantic, where broad and fertile acres awaited the industrious colonist, and where no penal laws interfered with the free exercise of their religion." To do so, however, even if advantageous, was impracticable. Love of native land was always the strongest passion of the Irish race. To separate from the home of their fathers was regarded by them as a calamity worse than death. To their minds there was no prize in any foreign land to compensate for the loss of their own. With persistency they clung to the sacred spot; even accepting the humiliating conditions imposed by the new masters, finding some solace in the hope that a just Providence would in His own time raise up a liberator and restore their ancient liberties.

The great majority of the population still continued to be of the native race and of the Catholic creed. Although powerful in numbers they were politically helpless. They were completely at the mercy of the foreign proprietors of the soil. They were barely tolerated as tenants at will, in constant dread of eviction, as the caprice of the landlord or his agent might dictate. Their relations with the landed gentry were those of the shark dealing with his prey.

The character of the men who represented British authority in Ireland had all the grossness of the long past feudal times when the animal instincts held sway and the passion of avarice steeled the heart against the cries of justice. The average landlord, as he was known in Ireland, was a libertine. The enormous revenues which he drew from his estates he squandered with lavish hand in his English castle or on the continent. Whenever he condescended to visit his Irish estates he kept aloof from the tenants as if his bad conscience made him dread some evil from the very people to whom he owed his wealth.

As those estates came into his hands by royal favor and by schemes of a questionable character he could not be expected to display any of the virtues of true nobility. His origin was often of the humblest character. He seemed to live only for the pleasure of extravagance and the grosser vices.

Conviviality would be a feeble name for his pastimes. He lived up to his revenues, and as the estate passed from father to son it showed no improvement. The son was usually more prodigal, more wasteful and reckless than the father. The estates became mortgaged, and as each succeeding owner surpassed the former in a life of debauch new debts were added to the old, until the whole property became bankrupt, or held in control of the courts for the benefit of creditors. This was the general condition of the landlord class, and such is the financial condition of most of the Irish estates at the present day.

Another part of the new foreign element in Ireland's population comprised a numerous body of government officials, such as judges, sheriffs, revenue officers, and such subsidized favorites of the civil administration attracted by the comfortable salaries and other emoluments which they contrived to extract from the country's revenues.

This class all owing its advancement to the favor of government found its interests identical with those of royalty. To keep the native peasantry in a state of helpless subjection and without a voice in legislation of any kind was their determined policy.

As the courts of law were constituted and maintained for those long centuries of foreign control a citizen of the native peasant class could not hope for just consideration in any legal dispute.

An appeal to the law was easy enough. The legal fraternity was on hand at every turn. The pomp, and circumstance, and ceremony of the bench was ready in abundance. But what a court! What a mockery of justice! Judge, jury, sheriff, clerk, liveried employees, even to the jailer and hangman, were all one with the omnipresent landed gentry, who might violate any law in dealing with the impoverished and hated native. Woe to the tenant who would have the audacity to enter litigation with his landlord!

Why enumerate the severities practised for several generations on this crushed people—the packed juries, the atrocities of petty tyrants in the shape of village magistrates, the ferocious passions of irresponsible jailers?

Opportunities for education were purposely denied to the peasantry. This was one of the heaviest grievances, and was felt most keenly by a people gifted with intelligence of a high order and passionately fond of learning. The list of wrongs presented in the records of those times might be extended to the point of weariness.

In other countries and in our own times, when courtesy and kindness is universally observed between all classes it is difficult to conceive the arrogant manners of the so-called gentry of Ireland towards the native peasantry.

Persons now living can go back in memory over a period of fifty years and vividly recall that haughty bearing and open contempt displayed by the dominant aristocracy for the humiliated race.

Even the tender youth on either side were primed with that bitter spirt of strife which they witnessed in the conduct of their elders. Wordy encounters were common in the streets as the well fed child of the aristocrat jeered at the native peasant school fellow and taunted him with his lowly condition.

Thus harassed in his adversities through several generations, the Irish peasant was liable to become irritable and suspicious in the course of an ordeal that no temperament, however genial, could sustain.

It would have been a miracle if a people so long and so grievously subjected to wrong and to insult should show no sign of impatience.

Their prolonged state of discontent aggravated by inability to discuss openly their ordinary rights gave rise to the various secret societies which were formed in the country from time to time.

Nor is it difficult to explain the occasional outbursts of passion and violence which the historian of those troubled times has to record.

Those who know the nature of the provocation in such cases will admit that patience was tried beyond the limit of human endurance, as it is understood in the most civilized and law-abiding communities.

It was through the influence of their religion alone, which taught patience in adversity and to return good for evil that they were able to submit to wrong for so many generations, and to bear their well-earned character of industrious and peaceable citizens.

From the foregoing it will be seen that the population of Ireland during the long period under review formed two hostile camps. To speak of an Irish question, or Irish agitation, was misleading. The expression was equivocal. There was the Ireland of the ancient race, and the Ireland of the foreign minority, owning the soil and constituting the civil power. The one was content with the existing conditions and the administration; the other yearned for a change that would relieve them from grievances next to intolerable.

What were called national movements for securing independent legislation were thwarted by a powerful faction not in reality a part of the Irish nation, but devoted to the private interests of an alien minority. The conditions still remain the same. The old difficulty of disunion is explained, and presents a problem that is not yet solved.

The other baneful source of discord planted in the country by British force was the Protestant creed. If no other object was intended but to excite animosity between neighboring races and perpetuate strife in a peaceful community this was the most efficient for that purpose that could be devised.

To force upon the people of Ireland a creed which they detested was, indeed, capping the climax of wrongs inflicted on them. It was sowing the seed of a bitter strife between the authority that assumed the task and the resisting people who repelled such wanton abuse on the part of the civil government.

We must bear in mind what this new attempt implied, as it was understood by the Irish people. It implied an outrage on their liberties, on their feelings, and on their intelligence. It was bad enough to deprive them of their civil rights by taking away all voice in their country's legislation. It was bad enough to have robbed them of their soil by various confiscations, but to try to invade their rights to mental freedom, their right to free deliberation and forming opinion on matters purely religious, was regarded as an impertinence to be resisted to the bitter end—even at the cost of life.

The continued refusal on the part of the people to accept the new religion answered the purposes of the government admirably. For rapacity found a pretext for new confiscations, while fines and forfeitures supplied additional revenues for the royal coffers. It suited equally a multitude of unscrupulous adventurers looking for plunder in the conquered provinces. A large class whose loyalty was always pliant and those greedy for land were ready to accept the rich prizes which the recusant Irish forfeited to the crown. Those of no particular mental convictions or conscientious scruples could put on the air of zeal for the King's prerogative, and with artful hypocrisy denounce the victims of the penal laws, always sure of ample reward for their services.

It would have been an easy matter to yield to force, to obey the arbitrary command without inquiring into the motive, or questioning the right of the ruler in the case. To accept the new creed, to profess in a brief sentence the loyalty that was exacted would be rewarded by secure possession of property and home, by advancement in a useful profession and luxurious ease. A mere equivocation, a set form of words, with indistinct, or doubtful meaning, would have pleased the inquisitorial court. But the Irish Catholic subject had higher aspirations than those of mere sordid gain that might be secured by betraying truth, or co-operating in wanton injustice.

It was one of the most tremendous experiments of physical force in conflict with moral resistance. The ordeal was dreadful for the whole Catholic population defending the right of conscience.

As an immovable rock in the midst of the ocean stands firm after repeated storms and the fury of raging billows dashing against it, so did the Irish people stand unflinching in their faith, resisting for centuries the furious assaults of heresy, and defying the wanton claims of human power over the rights of conscience and the independent exercise of deliberate reason.

They conquered at last; but their victory was one of the intellectual order; and they deserve the laurels due to true heroes in the cause of mental freedom for all future time. In the course of the tedious battle the disasters inseparable from such determined resistance were serious, and their material losses and grievances will long continue unrepaired.

The Irish Catholic people marshalled their ranks on the side of humanity and liberty. Their claim was that civil power has its proper limits—that there are eternal principles which no earthly monarch can alter—that the civil power, whether in the hands of royalty or other magistrate, however titled, cannot constrain the subject in the exercise of his mental faculties, especially in convictions on his future and eternal destiny. It was a stern defiance. The battle was waged by the recusant subject with fearful odds against him, and the whole world looked on with eager interest.

Contemporary peoples, long crushed under similar despotic claims of the civil power, held their breath in astonishment at this unheard of defiance of royal abuses, and awaited anxiously the victory so full of significance to all others oppressed for conscience sake.

The exercise of arbitrary authority in whatever hands and on whatever pretext, saw its doom not far off. The old stronghold of irresponsible despots claiming unquestioning obedience met an assault designed to shatter it from its foundations.

Who does not see here a contest of the greatest import to all mankind? Ireland was ready to reject the abstract claim to encroach on her intellectual freedom with a promptness and energy that would be unmistakable; but its abhorrence for this particular invasion of human rights in its concrete form was greater as the motives of government were base and disreputable.

The intense abhorrence entertained by the Irish people for this outrage offered them, and the length of time in which the hated policy of the government continued will explain the disasters that necessarily followed.

The new religion meant the submission of the mind to opinions formed by a voluptuous monarch who aspired to the role of a head of the church—nothing less than a sort of pope, to regulate what his subjects must believe.

This claim of the British government was kept up and enforced by every artifice that a despotic power or the depraved ingenuity of man could devise during the long period of three hundred years. It arose with the quarrel of Henry VIII. with the pope in 1527, and was not laid to rest until the abolition of the penal laws in 1829 through the agitation of the great O'Connell.

Fifteen different monarchs occupied the British throne during that period, and, if we except Mary's short reign of five years, there was no abatement in the odious warfare against the ancient religion of the Irish nation. As the different monarchs succeeded each other on the English throne the administration in Ireland differed only in the degree of severity with which those infamous laws were put in force.

The pretext alleged by the government for introducing the new doctrine and enforcing its acceptance under such severe penalties was to secure the loyalty of the subject.

If the Irish people could be led to believe that this was the real motive they would be open to argument and would listen with some degree of respect to the demands of royalty. But they knew it was only a pretext. It was enough for them to know the origin of the new creed. No plausible words could hide from them the plain fact that it had its birth in the depraved passions of Henry. The people refused to sanction Henry's domestic vicious career. Henry resolved on revenge, and determined to get rid of an authority that interfered with his enjoyments.

There is one characteristic of the Irish people that most historians overlook. It is this. They can tolerate other human passions with a degree of patience, but they have an insuperable abhorrence of that which made Henry put away his lawful wife and led him to become a shameless brute. Whatever may be the explanation of this trait in their character, they regarded this form of vice among those most deserving of contempt.

What wonder, therefore, if a religion coming from Henry would be eyed with suspicion by such a people? It was too plain to them that he was playing the part of the depraved boy who wanted to free himself from the authority of his good father in order to pursue his vicious course without restraint.

Besides the passion of lust at the bottom of the new religion, there was another which showed itself plainly from the very beginning.

It was that of disordered ambition and wounded pride, which saw a boundless field for its gratification in the overthrow of the pope's spiritual authority. Both of these passions betrayed themselves at once in the so-called reformer of Germany, from whom Henry got his new religious views.

But still further a third passion cropped up in Henry's new schemes. It was that of avarice. Once the profligate monarch gave himself up to the basest form of vice it was easy to foresee that other extremes would soon be adopted. His extravagance led to new demands for means to fill his depleted treasury. He looked about him for available sources of revenue. Why spare the rich monasteries and the incomes of the old church, whose bishops refused to accept him as a new pope? His mind was made up. Two of his unholy passions would be gratified by the same stroke.

He had no difficulty in finding among members of his court, in the officers of the army, and the government officials men of his own mind. They were ready as pliant tools to carry out his vast schemes of plunder in the numerous religious houses throughout the kingdom.

For the sake of appearances there were official inquiries made into the condition of the various communities—whether the monks were strict observers of their monastic rules. It was plainly for the interests of the King and of his deputies in carrying out these projects to discover and report abuses among the inmates.

The reports were, of course, unfavorable, just as the King had desired. Wholesale pillage of these homes of lax livers was at once commenced.

Before the eyes of the public the project was represented as a work of zeal, intended for the real good of the monks; an efficient way of correcting their frailties. For, even if they were driven out of their homes and robbed of their livings, it was eminently necessary for the edification of the Kingdom.

To avoid giving too much of a shock to the feelings of the people the smaller monasteries only were seized in the beginning. Gradually the larger prizes fell victims to the rapacity of the King's agents, who were amply rewarded with a portion of the spoils bestowed on them by their master for their zeal in his service.

The enormous income secured from this pillage of the numerous religious houses in England was enough to meet Henry's most extravagant demands. But why should he stop there once the profitable enterprise was set on foot. Why not make Ireland yield up her share in the great reformation of monastic morals?

As the bishops and abbots refused to acknowledge his supremacy in the church, he took revenge by issuing a decree for their deposition from office and the seizure of their revenues.

In May, 1541, by Henry's instructions, a parliament was summoned in Dublin under the Viceroy, Lord Grey. The object was to carry out the King's new policy, and force the whole Irish people to acknowledge his supremacy in ecclesiastical affairs, as well as to decide his claim to the title of King over the island.

This parliament was not representative of the Irish nation, as many of the most powerful Irish chiefs took no part in it. Its members were old dependents and agents of the crown, mostly residents of the Pale, and selected under the Viceroy's supervision on account of their well-known sympathy with England's interests. However, they did as their royal master desired. By a so-called parliamentary decree Henry was declared King of Ireland and head of the church.

The Irish bishops rejected with scorn the

novel pretensions of the licentious King. All the consequences followed just as had lately occurred in England. The Irish dioceses were placed in the hands of men of pliant conscience, whose ambition was more for filthy lucre than the purity of truth.

Among the Irish ecclesiastics there were found a few who became apostates during the trying ordeal, purchasing the temporary dignities offered at the price of their eternal interests. The property of the religious orders that had been established for generations in every section of the country was seized by royal order, while the monks and other clergy were expelled, many put to death by the military sent to evict them, or forced to fly for shelter to the continent.

Here was the beginning of that huge robbery under the name of religion committed in Ireland by order of British monarchs.

A motley crowd of fortune hunters from England were ready for the spoils. Hypocrites abounded in these days. A door was opened to human depravity, which is never wanting when encouraged by opportunities. As the King himself defied the plainest laws of morality no wonder if common subjects equally unscrupulous were eager to grasp at stolen prizes offered for apostacy. What a prince can do with unblushing dissimulation will cease to appear shameful in the eyes of pliant subjects under the influence of avarice.

A selection of such hirelings were planted

by Henry as his own bishops to take charge of the old faithful dioceses of Ireland, while other adaventurers from across the channel were rewarded for their loyalty with the rich estates confiscated from the monasteries.

After Henry's death the spoliation went on with increased vigor under the boy king, Edward VI. and Elizabeth.

Soon after the latter ascended the throne a packed parliament was convened in England for the purpose of declaring the Protestant religion established in the Kingdom.

In this was enacted the famous law requiring all seeking to enter any civil or ecclesiastical office to take the test oath, which was as follows: "I. N. N. do hereby testify and declare, in my conscience, that the Queen's highness is the only supreme governor of this realm, as well in spiritual and ecclesiastical things and causes as in temporal."

In Ireland, especially, this test was rigorously put in force.

A foreign clergy was imposed upon the country with the object of converting the inhabitants to the new faith as by English law established. In every part of the country the people saw planted in their midst those strange intruders with the titles of bishop or minister richly subsidized with the spoils of the ancient church.

To the Irish people this body of pampered ecclesiastics were as far from edifying as could be imagined. As representing the Church of

Christ it was a broad satire—a joke to make the peasantry split their sides with laughter, if the humorous view of the case was not overshadowed by the feeling of disgust which they had for the would-be preachers.

They had read enough of Scripture to know that a genuine minister of Christ must give proof of some self-denial in his own life such as the divine Master inculcates. The new pastors sent over by Henry and Elizabeth had no such qualities to recommend them. These sleek ministers backed up by royal authority, enjoying princely salaries, housed in elegant mansions, with the choicest glebe lands as an extra perquisite, consoled by charming wives and a numerous offspring, displaying a taste for luxury as if it were a necessary part of their profession, and with arrogance of manner whenever they ventured to appear in public, were hardly the sort of men to gain the respect or the confidence of the native Irish. The contrast was too great between their sumptuous style of living and the simple religious life of the monks and other clergy who had been banished or put to death to make room for them. Even the simplest peasant could not be blindfolded in this. If the objection to the monks consisted in the extent of their wealth, or in carelessness regarding the monastic rule, there was no sign of improvement in those sent to take their place. The Church of England bishop or parson was notoriously and everywhere a man devoted to his own personal comfort, insatiable in collecting his tithes, and showing a haughty contempt for the poor, with no apparent object in life except to feast sumptuously every day.

Such a church organization was to all the Irish people a glaring imposture and was regarded with supreme contempt. It meant to them a two-fold burden, which they were bound to resist with eternal hatred. It represented the foreign civil power which robbed them of their lands and their liberties. At the same time ,pretending to be a church aiming at a reform of their ancient faith, it represented a huge and shameless lie under the sanctimonious mask of religion.

It was supported by the civil power in order to devour the country's vitals, and to be the instrument in turn of perpetuating that power in enslaving the nation.

To witness a colony of parsons enjoying the stolen goods of the people while pretending a mission to reform that people's faith—that was the climax of effrontery. A child could see that it was the estates and revenues they were after.

What language could describe the disasters brought upon Ireland by this new colony of hypocrites and the harassing measures used to impose on the people the new creed!

For three hundred years a barbarous code of penal laws were put in force against all who refused to accept it. Confiscation of estates for such refusal was one of the most ordinary inflictions.

Imprisonment and heavy fines for attending Catholic worship continued a steady source of exasperation to the great body of the inhabitants. The Catholic nobility were one by one stripped of their possessions, and either forced into exile or to remain in a state of destitution.

The reign of Elizabeth presents the most complete picture of the extreme severity employed by the civil power in Ireland to compel the people to obedience in spiritual matters. The horrors of brutal force used against freedom of conscience drew the attention of the civilized world.

Elizabeth's chief hobby seems to have been that all should acknowledge her as the head of the church. To deny her that prerogative was taken as the most serious insult that could be offered. Her wounded ambition must be vindicated at all hazards. She could never relent in her fixed determination to visit the recusants with the heaviest penalties.

Other monarchs who meddled in the religious question were as cruel as she proved herself to be, but her name is associated more prominently with those Irish atrocities for which she was willingly responsible. The great length of her reign,too, gave her full opportunity for the display of her character in its true colors. Her iron rule lasted forty-four years; and during that long period the fierce struggle was kept up in Ireland, and the devastation of the country went on, accompanied by barbarities of the grossest kind committed by her troops to force her religious views on an unwilling people.

Some historians disliked to call her measures cruel. Even our own usually fairminded Bancroft, when referring to her policy at that period, uses the word "firmness," while he uses the word "bigoted" in reference to Philip King of Spain, although the measures employed by the Spanish ruler were the same as those adopted by Elizabeth, and both on pretence of religion. The impartial observer will pronounce such measures as cruel and heartless, whether perpetrated by Elizabeth or Philip of Spain, and equally deserving the reprobation of every civilized people.

To give one instance out of a thousand: When the Catholic Archbishop O'Hurley was tortured in Dublin in the year 1583 with the sanction of the Queen for the so-called crime of denying her spiritual supremacy his executioners placed his feet in tin boots filled with oil, under which a fire was kindled as a means of causing intense agony, we hardly think the sufferer would believe the word "firmness" the right expression to designate a certain quality in Elizabeth's character.

For similar reasons, no doubt, certain historians would explain in mild language the conduct of Oliver Cromwell at Drogheda when he burned several hundred persons, including women and children, in the church where they took refuge from his fury.

Elizabeth's reign was also noted in Ireland as the period of the "priest-hunter." The class of spy known in Ireland under this title was created and fostered in the enforcement of the penal laws. To understand his peculiar calling we need only be reminded that the hardest of these laws were directed against the Catholic clergy. As they rejected with scorn the Queen's blasphemous claim they were ordered to leave the Kingdom under pain of death. A similar punishment was decreed for any one harboring a priest or bishop. This law was carried out with the utmost rigour. The clergy, whether monks or secular priests, were literally pursued with fire and sword. The military sent to complete their extermination, got full license to employ a variety of tortures as they might see fit in dealing with their victims. Most of them fled to the continent, while many hundreds were put to death. Out of one thousand Dominican monks residing in their convents in Ireland at the time of Henry's apostacy there were only four left at Elizabeth's death. The Franciscans fared in the same manner.

In the midst of this desolation and in the face of the greatest perils there were always some zealous priests to remain in the country under various disguises secretly visiting their faithful flocks in order to administer whatever consolations their religion could give under the circumstances.

That the penal law against them might have its effect, a high price was offered by public authority as a reward for the discovery of any such ecclesiastic in the country. Here was the field for the informer known in the language of the period as the "priest hunter." They were a vile class of men, and their number grew to be formidable, while exceedingly zealous for the Queen's dignity. A reign of terror prevailed in every corner of the island. Neither the obscure peasant's cottage nor the natural caves in the unfrequented mountainous regions was a safe retreat from these prowling demons in human shape. The scaffold was erected at every military post. The blood of the innocent was poured out day after day. Native Irish of the highest rank as well as the quiet peasantry were dragged to death for the so-called "treason" of openly professing their faith.

To pass through an ordeal of this kind that was prolonged, with very brief intervals of moderation, through fifteen successive reigns, was enough to demoralize any people. Joined to the horrors of persecution for conscience sake in the form of physical inflictions, decimation of families by execution, banishment, confiscation of property, the inhabitants were in a constant turmoil of controversy, bitter reproaches and irritating recriminations, as between the favored alien settler and the crushed and conquered natives.

If discontent is justly deemed the source of revolutions, here was a perpetual nursery of sullen plots and agitation with a vengeance.

Generations growing up amidst such influences will necessarily acquire an irritable temperament, mutual suspicions will become habitual, while a certain harshness will mingle with the most amiable disposition.

A thorough knowledge of the relations between the classes in Ireland will give the reasons of the tendency to disunion whenever popular attempts were made to remedy the nation's wrongs.

Whatever degree of impatience we are forced to witness in the character of the people can be traced to the same source—a long-continued brutal oppression borne with sullen defiance and undying resolve for revenge.

That brutal force has vanquished the weaker side, and enjoyed its victory for a long season will be the judgment of a superficial world. Unscrupulous arrogance and perfidy triumphs over justice and humanity.

But the Irish people in the midst of their defeat and humiliation represent another kind of victory in the cause of fidelity and the emancipation of the human mind. The power and the victory they represent is that of the soul— a power—a force that can prove itself invincible against the most formidable armies in its aspirations for truth and independence.

Reflecting philanthropists of our times can look back and discover in their unflinching adhesion to truth and their resolve to abolish all wanton claims of the civil ruler, under whatever form of dictatorship, a priceless victory for liberty to be secured in future times and in every nation.

During the very period under consideration here another people on the great American continent were engaged in a similar conflict, refusing to obey the unwarranted mandates of pampered royalty on the British throne.

The spirit that animated both was the same. Human liberty was approaching its full development, and human rights were about to reach a clearer definition. Who will refuse to these two nations struggling with despotism the gratitude due to their heroic persistency?

Through them the old narrow view of political rights made way for those broad ideas of popular independence and noble free institutions in which we all share in these modern times, and which are yet destined to reach a more perfect development.

The censure of disloyalty could not be charged to the Irish people in their protracted struggle with the abuses of royalty. The Irish rather erred in their too great fidelity to monarchs who were far from being worthy of their confidence. They poved their conscientious loyalty to Charles I. and James II. even at the risk of the greatest disaster to their country. If they had abandoned the cause of those worthless princes their own interests would have been assured.

With that scrupulous fidelity nurtured by the religion which they professed they cheerfully adhered to the cause of the rightful heir to the throne, as the laws of nations were then understood, and in matters relating to civil obedience; following the plain teaching of St. Paul to be obedient to the civil ruler for conscience sake, and the similar mandate of the Divine Master to give to Caesar what belongs to Caesar. But they, among all other nations, most emphatically insisted that the civil ruler can compel obedience only within certain limits—that there is a domain in which the secular authority must not presume to venture—the exercise of the powers of the mind, the convictions of the intellect in the relations between the individual and his Creator.

In a word, the Irish people have always been conspicuous and gained the admiration of the world for their valor in the material conflict of arms, while their unflinching fidelity to the principles of justice and intellectual freedom claims the respect of all who can appreciate civil and religious liberty.

CONCLUDING HINTS.

A question very natural will present itself to readers of history such as the foregoing. It is. Can we conceive a way of totally eradicating the spirit of rebellion from among the people of Ireland or any other people having similar grievances?

We answer without hesitation, it is not only possible, but it is easy to accomplish such a happy result.

It will come when statesmen are able to grasp the extent of those grievances and honestly inquiring into their cause, make haste to apply the remedies.

It is useless to hide from ourselves the fact that every discontented people point to certain adverse legislation, or to certain privileged classes among their fellow citizens as responsible for the evils of which they complain.

Whether the people are right, whether they have just grounds for judging harshly either of a system of government or of the powerful classes on whom they are wholly dependent deserves at least a serious inquiry.

It would seem that self-interest ought to induce such favored classes to promote the wellbeing of the classes depending upon them.

Judging from past history and the unaccountable stupidity or indifference of those in high places, when the wretchedness of multitudes cried out for relief, we still fear that the remedy will not come from the quarter whence the evils arise.

As long as human nature remains what it is and what the experience of ages has sadly taught—as long as it continues to be selfish, grasping, avaricious even to blindness to the miseries of fellowmen, we can hardly hope for that well balanced justice dictated even by self interest among the powerful individual citizens in dealing with the dependent classes. Even the old adage so intelligible to all, that the goose that lays the golden egg should not be killed, is too often forgotten.

When ordinary human compassion for the miseries of others who happen to be in our power is wanting, we would expect that the motive of private interest—of future profit, would lead those in power to pursue a clement and gentle policy. But, however the problem may be explained, the strong arm of the state must often be called upon to restrain the individual citizen in his ill advised or harsh dealings with a weaker brother.

Legislation must step in to regulate contracts and conditions of a private nature which affect the general well-being of the community. When statesmen can bring themselves to admit that the industrial classes, which form the majority in every civilized nation, have a right to a reasonable share of the fruit of their own industry—a right to protection in the enjoyment of their hard earned possessions—a right to the common blessings held out by a beneficent Providence to the industrious tiller of the soil—a right to be sustained in all his legitimate aspirations for advancement—then will government rest secure from the threats of discontented millions, and from the warnings, the sullen conspiracies of the agitator.

The solution of the so-called great problem is simple. Encourage industry by securing to the industrious the fruit of his toil. Let him see that nothing will impede his advancement when he devotes his energies to any laudable pursuit. Respect his private convictions, whether religious or political, and hinder not his free profession of them, as long as they have no dangerous tendencies.

This does not imply anything revolutionary. If there exists a nobility or a class of citizens powerful on account of the great wealth which they enjoy, let their rights be also respected equally with those of the common multitude. The public interests of the community will not demand from them the surrender of the dignity belonging to their position, or the possessions they legitimately acquired.

Limit them only in their power of doing wrong. When they employ their superior influence and wealth against the interests of the great masses of the community; when they abuse their power over the dependent classes so as to discourage industry, crush healthy ambition, stand in the way of private enterprise, then public legislation must step in and set limits to the mischief which such abuses inflict on the multitude.

It is not in Ireland alone that the stupid indifference of the powerful classes to the miseries of the dependent multitudes has brought its own punishment with it. The continent has had its share of horrors produced by like causes.

Reasonable concessions made by those in high places to their inferiors seldom pass unacknowledged. A generous policy on the part of the capitalist in dealing with the laborer turns out advantageous to both. The return of gratitude for fair treatment is hardly ever wanting among the employed towards the employer.

Why crush all hope in the heart of the laborer while he pursues a reasonable gain—a legitimate advancement?

Public policy—the prosperity of the nation demands that the causes of discontent shall be removed. If it exists the state should apply the remedy even to secure its own safety.

These general principles are never out of date. They apply at present as they did in past times, and there is no form of government that can afford to neglect them.

The humane and liberal spirit that has grown so general in all enlightened nations of our times inspires us with hope for the establishment of order and good will between the different classes of society. The great mistakes of governments and of the privileged classes will hardly be repeated.

The grave lessons of the past will be neglected at the peril of society now no less than in former times.

Until these lessons, taught us at such a fearful cost, are well learned and the mistakes of the past corrected let no one be surprised at revolutions.

www.ingramcontent.com/pod-product-compliance
Lightning Source LLC
Chambersburg PA
CBHW030332170426
43202CB00010B/1097